CHEEKY
WALKS

IN
BRIGHTON
& SUSSEX

**Written and researched
by
Tim Bick
David Bramwell
John Ashton**

Cheeky Walks in Brighton & Sussex

Comments/cut-price shiatsu: david@cheekyguides.com
Business enquiries/ego massage: tim@cheekyguides.com

ISBN 978-0956130310
First published in 2012 by Cheekyguides Ltd
Europa House, Goldstone Villas, Brighton BN3 3RQ
Revised and updated 2015
www.cheekyguides.com

Contributors

'Plaque To Plaque' is almost entirely the work of Ric Morris, a man who just gives and gives without complaint, even when you send him to Newhaven. 'Walking With Werewolves' is a route originally devised and written by Martine McDonagh. 'Groovin' in the Ghost Village' is from the first album by Grasscut. 'A Very British Walk' is partly based on a route by Eliza Skelton and her pug Ernie.

Gratitude is owed to our route testers, without whom several sets of directions would have landed you in Skegness:
Peter & Lisa; Count Fettucini & Yael; Rachel, Ros, Serena, Jinpa, Carina & Harry, Colleen, Peter, Judy, Tim & Sue, Ric & John, Tom & Dan; Mr Pipes, Colette, Fran, Charlotte & Christine, Kathleen & Ivan, Sarah & Ben, Rick, Penny, Nat, Anna, Andy, Pepe, Anika, Denise and Lisa.

Particular thanks to LJ, who walked a host of routes single-legged, and to Ric Morris for his insight and rucksack full of stories. We recommend his guided tours of Brighton at www.onlyinbrighton.co.uk. Ginormous thank yous to Jo for walking more routes than you can shake a walking stick at and listening to all the complaining.

Illustrations by the very talented Badaude.
For more information: www.badaude.typepad.com

Edited by Nicky Falkof, a woman of wise words.

Photo credits

Ric Morris pp 20, 51, 52, 98; Rick Webber pp 26, 56, 81; John Woodhams pp 13,48; Peter Chrisp p49; Penny Morgan p55; Tom Hume p57; Dan Hume p85.

About the Authors

David Bramwell

Raised in the wilds of Yorkshire, David is an experienced rambler, having scaled Mam Tor, walked the Peaks and completed the gruelling 40-mile Lyke Wake Walk in one day. Mind you, that was in 1987. Nowadays he can be found traipsing over the Downs in unsuitable trousers, trying to remember where he parked his Renault Clio.

Tim Bick

Utilising a perambulatory method that is brisk, resolute and positively rude at times, Tim has walked internationally, even when other forms of transport were readily available. His Swiss walking shoes are the envy of his colleagues, embodying style, practicality and the actions of a man with more spare cash than sense.

John Ashton

Covering 80 yards with a single stride, John thinks nothing of strolling to Grimsby and back in an afternoon, though his poor sense of direction means he often ends up in Poundland. He models himself on the legendary walkers' guide author Alfred Wainwright, except, unlike Wainwright, he's still alive and is allergic to tweed.

Contacting Cheeky Guides

These walks have been thoroughly tested by ourselves and a plethora of heroic volunteers, but should you have any difficulties (or, equally, want to tell us how much you enjoyed them) go to:
www.cheekyguides.co.uk/contact or Twitter @cheekybrighton

Why not become one of our special friends who we never unfriend on Facebook and share your photos at www.facebook.com/CheekyGuides

INTRODUCTION

If all you desire from a local walk is a dose of fresh air and a field of slightly stained sheep, you probably don't need this book. Should you like your stroll spiced up with a little adventure, a dab of mischief and a pocketful of intriguing stories, then you're on the right page. Here are 21 unique themed walks, in town, country, or a bit of both. There are art, alleyway and sex trails, plus rambles that retrace the final steps of master criminals and suicidal novelists. Some walks feature special activities, such as a musical accompaniment around a ghost village or a night time wander by the light of the moon. For the casual weekend visitor (or Woody Allen types who feel "at two with nature"), there are short urban walks in and around Brighton that can be polished off in an hour or two, while the inveterate rambler will also find plenty of routes further afield, though you won't have to go beyond Arundel. Naturally, the Cheeky commentary packs in plenty of salient facts and silly trivia along the way.

While themed, each walk in this book has been carefully created to be a pleasure in its own right. You don't really need to be a football fan to enjoy our Albion Trail – it may take in Brighton's football stadiums past and present but also incorporates a national lilac collection, woodland trails, quiet villages and a chance to visit Toys R Us on the Old Shoreham Road. And as we're mixing up the urban and rural in this book, yes, there is the occasional eyesore. There are stretches of our route through Newhaven that would have Prince Charles weeping into his herbal tea, but where else would you find a walk dedicated to the elusive Lord Lucan? In fact the only thing this book does not contain are 18-mile hikes, because those are the ones nobody ever does unless they're on a school trip led by a sadistic geography teacher.

HOW TO USE THIS BOOK

All of our walks bar one are accessible by public transport, with clear instructions on how to get there and back. They have also been designed to work without a map. But don't let us stop you carrying one if it makes you feel more secure. While there are refreshment stops along the way or at the end it never does any harm to take the odd can of fizzy Ribena and a cream horn with you, in case you get lost in the wilderness of Hove.

The opening page of each walk covers the important stuff. Key symbols are explained below.

 How to reach the start of the walk. For Brighton walks you will need to know the location of Brighton Station, the Clock Tower (directly halfway between the station and the sea) and Churchill Square (50 yards uphill from the Clock Tower).

 Approximate length in miles and hours.

 Where it starts and ends. This might seem obvious to *you*, but we get letters you know.

 Where to park your car and what gear to leave it in.

 What it's like underfoot and whether your scarlet winklepickers will survive the experience.

 Special things to look out for.

 This covers all health and safety issues, from nettle rash to alien abduction. But for heaven's sake, please don't take it seriously.

 A recommended movie that complements the theme of the walk, to be viewed afterwards when you're home with the foot spa and a packet of Garibaldi.

 Walks where you're advised to carry a firearm. To be honest this symbol isn't used in *this* book, but can be found in our forthcoming Life-Threatening Walks in North Manchester.

VITALLY IMPORTANT UPDATES

Time is not always a healer – all known changes to directions and sights in these walks can be found at www.cheekyguides.co.uk/walkupdates

THE BRIGHTON WALKS

THE SUSSEX WALKS

BOOZY BACKSTREETS OF
BRUNSWICK

Built from scratch early in the 19th century (like Milton Keynes but without the concrete cows), Brunswick was once an entirely separate town complete with its own railway station, market and town hall. It boasted some of the city's finest architecture, regal squares and a wealth of pubs which make up the backbone of this walk-cum-drunken weave. If nine watering holes in one walk seem excessive, think yourself lucky you didn't have to do this 150 years ago when there were over fifty in the very same streets. The notion of visiting every pub on the way should be viewed as an option rather than a challenge, by the way. If you fancy visiting the clock shop and Buddhist retreat along the way then it might be best to keep off the sauce altogether – they're unlikely to appreciate you knocking things over whilst serenading all and sundry with an off-key version of 'We Are The Champions'. Drunk or sober, you'll find these sleepy roads that straddle the Brighton and Hove border a pleasure to explore. If you're still able to stand you'll finish with a viewing of Brunswick's stunning seafront architecture. Astonishingly, the centrepiece Regency squares were almost demolished in the 1950s by Hove Town Council, before organised public opposition saved them. Fittingly, a few decades later Hove Council was demolished instead.

 From the Clock Tower go down West Street to the seafront and turn right. Regency Square is 500 yards away on the right

 1.5 miles/2 to 24 hours dependent on your drinking habits

 Regency Square, opposite the West Pier and the iSore

 Pavement all the way, so put on your two-tone town brogues

 The Lion and Lobster's outdoor 'indoor' room, anchovy-flavoured vodka

 Drunkenly arranging to run away to Algeria with the landlady at The Farm Tavern 38%

 Jeffrey Bernard Is Unwell

① We begin our constitutional opposite the rusty remains of the West Pier. If you're planning on 'making an evening of it' and haven't already lined your stomach, we recommend a fish supper here at either the Regency or the adjacent Melrose.

Regency Square's well-to-do residents were unamused by the building of the West Pier in 1866 since it blocked their sea view. A hundred or so years later they were clamouring for its restoration. There's no pleasing some people. The square retains considerable beauty, despite the indignity of the underground car park imposed by witless town planners, and the oppressive shadow cast by the i360. In the 19th century Oscar Wilde marmalised the garden railings here by crashing his horse and carriage, later describing it as 'an accident of no importance'. Today it's home to two of the city's more unusual hotels, the Pelirocco and Artists Residence, both with rooms designed by artists, pop stars and urbanites.

② Walk west along the seafront and take the fourth turning on the right, Oriental Place. Halfway up on the right is the Oriental Hotel and its swanky little bar.

A good place for a cocktail opening salvo, this tends to only be open on Friday and Saturday nights, along with Wednesday and Thursday evenings in the summer. It's also the former location of the Brighton Belle nightclub where Fatboy Slim used to wave his pants at the small but appreciative crowd. You might need to ring the bell to get let in, but it's worth it to spread yourself out on some giant velour lips in this twinkly little nook.

③ At the top of Oriental Place, hang a left along Silwood Street past Belchers Café and continue to the Lion and Lobster on your right.

Known as The Rockingham until 1988, this pub caused consternation amongst local residents when the name change was accompanied by a garish pink coat of paint. These days it's a traditional seaside boozer complete with psychedelic beer-stained carpets, seafaring tales from salty old dogs and a multi-storey warren of rooms.

④ Turn right by the Lion and Lobster into Bedford Place then next left into Norfolk Square, which becomes Cross Street as you proceed. After a hundred yards the Robin Hood pub appears on your right.

The label on the building proclaiming this a "people's pub" is no mere marketing slogan, since all the profits made here go to local charities. This UK first is thanks to the munificence of Martin Webb, who made his millions in the trendy Brighton pub makeover boom of the 90s. They keep their ales well here, and there's an abundance of intimate corners to snuggle into, as well as a healthy selection of board games. If you want to start a row with your partner we recommend playing the board version of the ancient TV quiz show Mr & Mrs.

⑤ Continue along Cross Street, stopping to peruse number 15, the clock shop.

The road used to be known locally as Clock Street, such was the abundance of chronographic businesses, but now there is only the one. This place is a precious curio, much like the stock, being part of the vanishing breed of funny old Brighton shops run by unfathomable shopkeepers. Rather than the anticipated cacophony of tick-tocks you're greeted instead by a deathly silence from the venerable timepieces that fill every corner. An encounter with the owner may be just as unsettling, some days eliciting no more than a sigh and other times a sudden enthusiasm for revealing such details as the fact that his upstairs room used to be a knocking shop.

⑥ Carry on to the end of Cross Street where you take a left down Waterloo Street, past the gateway to the Old Market and on to the Iron Duke Hotel near the bottom of the street.

Boasting the rightful title of 'Brighton's Most Haunted', The Iron Duke is a classic local boozer

with a typical cast of eccentric regulars, personable staff and the obligatory opinionated builder propping up the bar. As for its spectral patrons, there's the angry man in the cellar, the freaky woman and baby in room two and a spooky ginger cat. In fact you can even buy a DVD made here by the Paranormal Investigation Group (PIGS), who just happen to be a bunch of ex-coppers.

⑦ Hang a right next to the pub down Brunswick Street East, following it around and up. The small houses here are typical of those constructed for tradesmen and servants of the grand mansions in places like Brunswick Square, which backs onto this road on the left. On the right as you approach the next road junction is the Old Market, now a venue but once the market hall built to serve Brunswick Town. With remarkable foresight it came complete with its own sewer out to the sea, decades before even London had any sort of sewerage system. Continue to the top of the road and our next destination, The Paris House on the corner with Western Road.

In an attempt to chime with one of Brighton's most popular career choices, this pub's previous name was The Juggler. In a break with Western Road tradition this is now a distinctly salubrious

establishment, and as pasted on as the French theme may be, they do a mean cheese platter and some rather tasty ciders and beers from across la Manche.

⑧ Go straight uphill, crossing Western Road and the length of Cambridge Road. At the top on the other side of the road is the Bodhisattva Centre. If you can still see how many fingers you're holding up this is our next destination.

Formerly Wick Lodge, this 200-year old building has served as a convent, private boys' school, and one of England's biggest squats back in the 90s. The grounds span an incredible (for the centre of Brighton) two acres which incorporate a peace garden, play area and vegetable patch. Don't be afraid to walk up the drive and have a look around as Buddhists are a welcoming bunch, and run an excellent veggie café.

⑨ From the top of Cambridge Road head west and take the second left turning, Farm Road. Pop into the Farm Tavern on your right.

*Having survived for decades without much alteration, the Farm finally succumbed to a makeover in 2015. Upstairs is actually now nicer than before. As for downstairs - well, the colour selection is a bit **sudden**. There is some compensation for the loss of atmosphere in the form of gluten-free roast dinners, if you're one of those people who just can't bear the taste of gluten.*

⑩ A mere amble downhill brings you to the miniscule Cooper's Cask.

If you forgot to eat earlier then you're in luck here, and the Sunday roasts are among the best in town. Being such a tiny pub, however, during busy periods you may find yourself eating your nut roast off your knees in the gents' toilets.

⑪ At the bottom of Farm Road cross over and turn right down Western Road. Take the first left into Brunswick Street West and look for the Bow Street Runner on your right.

This street feels like a scene from an old Ealing Studios film, with its mix of quaint old houses, oily workshops, garages and a proper local free of gaming machines and Sky TV. The pub's name was changed from the Station Inn when they got fed up with all the telephone train enquiries. This is actually a true story.

⑫ Proceed downhill and take the next right where Brunswick Street West suffers an identity crisis and splits into two. At the next road, Lansdowne Place, go left and then first right to Alice Street. At the end on your left lies your final drinking establishment, the Brunswick. Those on the pub crawl may choose to stay here for the rest of the evening, playing Shove Piggy Shove, trying to chat up a pot plant and then quietly falling asleep on the floor of the toilets around midnight. Those of you doing a more sober version of this walk may continue to the last part.

The last refurb here was, we think, intended to be 'American', if the mahogany flavour Venetian blinds are any guide. Step into their live music room, though, and you'll find much of their lovely 1930s wood panelling still intact, plus there's plenty of entertainment on offer most nights of the week with a leaning towards jazz and blues.

⑬ Make for the seafront and initially go right for fifty yards in order to admire the splendour of Adelaide Crescent. Return to the south end of Holland Road

and continue east half a mile back to Regency Square.

The top of Adelaide Crescent opens into Palmeira Square, which in 1833 was the site of the Anthaeum, a stupendous 65-foot high glass dome that was to contain exotic trees and birds. Unfortunately some bright spark decided it would look nicer without the central supporting pillar, and like a badly set blancmange the structure collapsed in a heap just weeks before it was due to open. It was another twenty years before anyone got round to clearing away the wreckage. On the way back you'll pass by the custard-coloured Brunswick Terrace and Square, the seafront's only remaining green space courtesy of Hove Lawns, and the Art Deco linearity of Embassy Court, once home to Terence Rattigan and Keith Waterhouse. Look out too for the restored bandstand and the angel statue, next to which is the always-open Meeting Place café where you can collapse with a Lucozade and a flapjack. Even if it's Christmas Day.

DAVID ROSEN
confused customers here
1988-2004

Dali model
DRAKO
waxed his moustache here
1992-2011

PLAQUE TO PLAQUE

NICK CAVE
crashed his Jag here
2010

THE MAN WHO WAVED AT BUSES
waved here
1976-2008

Being London's playground and retreat for a couple of hundred years has allowed Brighton to attract plenty of colourful people: politicians, writers, scientists, non-conformists, the French, terrorists and even Leo Sayer. Many of them have been honoured with their own little gift to posterity, a monumental plaque. This promenade leads you to many of those dotted around central Brighton, each one revealing a tasty morsel of Brighton's diverse history and culture. This is a short easy walk with plenty of Lanes and seafront action, punctuated with a nose inside some big hotels, and makes a great introduction to the city's more outré characters, unsung heroes, villains and posh nobs. As well as covering some of the core themes of the city – innovation, art, music, alcohol, dodgy therapies and feisty dykes – it uncovers lesser-known juicy bits for even the most Brighton-savvy.

From the Clock Tower go down North Street. At the mini-roundabout turn left into Pavilion Buildings

1.5 miles/1.5 hours

Begins at Pavilion Buildings, finishes at Holiday Inn on the seafront

Easy flat pavement

Couples having illicit rendezvous in hotel lobbies

Depression from comparing plaque-worthy celebrities to today's Brighton celebrities 87%

The Magic Box

① Standing outside the Royal Pavilion Shop at the end of Pavilion Buildings, admire the Guajarati-style Indian gateway.

A plaque here recalls that the gateway was a gift from the people of India in thanks for giving the Pavilion over as a hospital for Indian soldiers injured on the Western Front. On the wall to its right you can still make out the original carved inscription.

② Head back to North Street crossing over onto East Street and past the taxi rank. The street opens to a square on the right. Walk to the far right hand corner and look for a stone plaque by the door of Fishy Fishy. Be brave and enter the glass porch they've stuck on the front of the building for our next plaque.

Martha Gunn was a legendary 'dipper', a fisherman's wife who administered therapeutic sea bathing by forcing terrified aristocrats beneath the waves. She became a friend of the Prince Regent and didn't retire until the age of 86. The fish-cum-celebrity tradition continues, with her house now a fish restaurant owned by Dermot O'Leary.

③ Go across the square back to East Street and turn right towards the sea. After a short distance the pedestrian section ends and you turn left into a

broad alleyway which opens out to the Old Steine. Turn left again, go a few doors along and find the plaque to Maria Fitzherbert on the YMCA building (for more information see the Sex and the City walk). Cross the multiple lane road east to the verdant centre of the Steine and the fountain. Look for the plaque by the south side base of the fountain.

Old Steine was once the social hub of Brighton. The number of plaques here is testimony to the concentration of sought-after properties that overlooked the Steine, and also to the fact that poor people don't get much of a mention in history books. There's a curious plaque in the flowerbed, courtesy of Fountain International, a Brighton-based (where else?) organisation promoting peace and healing through Earth energies, tofu and gargling.

④ Fortified by the Earth energies, head to the buildings on the south side of Old Steine. Cross the road to the youth hostel that was once the Royal York Hotel, which proudly sports a blue plaque.

After the excesses of his brother George IV, King William IV's reign was marked with dutiful sobriety, "never drinking above a pint of sherry before dinner". William's great-great-great-great grandson (from his affair with an Irish actress) is none other than celebrity toff David Cameron.

⑤ Cross to the east side of Old Steine in line with the pier and head north with the buildings on your right, looking for numbers 30 and 20.

Sir Edward Marshall Hall was a barrister known as 'The Great Defender' for his passionate defence in some of the most notorious Victorian murder cases. He once implored a jury, "Look at her, gentlemen... God never gave her a chance – won't you?" Gideon Mantell was a pioneering palaeontologist who first identified the Iguanodon from fossils near Cuckfield. Well done that man!

⑥ Turn right up St James's Street for a few hundred yards. On the corner of Madeira Place on the right is St James Tavern with a plaque.

Tuaca is an Italian liqueur ('vanilla and citrus') which, like many of the town's residents, is 35% alcohol and has found a unique affinity with Brighton. The landlord fell in love with the niche-marketed Tuaca while on holiday in Colorado and started selling it in St James Tavern. It's now sold in most pubs in central Brighton, but almost nowhere else in the UK. Go on, have a shot.

⑦ Head right down Madeira Place. Turn right at the end and cross the road towards the sea at the lights. Turn right and follow the pavement round the Sea Life Centre in a semi-circle, cross the road again to the pier and proceed west for a few yards. Cross the main road back to the Royal Albion Hotel at the crossing.

On the Royal Albion Hotel, immediately facing you as you cross the road, is a stone plaque to Dr Richard Russell. From his house here the doctor prescribed sea bathing to treat almost any illness – including cancer, madness, and fear of seawater – and is credited as the man who first put Brighton on the map. "If you seek his monument, look around" says his plaque, although if you look around now his legacy appears to be four lanes of traffic jams and a gang of lads from Croydon. Also on the Royal Albion Hotel to the left is a plaque to William Gladstone, four times Prime Minister.

⑧ With the buildings on your right, walk along the seafront road for about 200 yards until you get to the concrete and glass block that is the Waterfront Hotel. Enter the hotel, taking the stairs on the right which bring you to the gargantuan central atrium. Debate whether the building looks better from the inside and then head to the exit on the opposite side of the atrium. Walk straight ahead with the pillared town hall on your right and look for a blue plaque on it just round the corner.

In 1774 workmen were digging the foundation excavations for a new market hall on the site of the former chapel and priory of St Bartholomew's Grange. Finding a cemetery, they downed tools out of respect for the dead. Until, that is, a local vicar informed them that the monks had been Catholics, at which point they immediately resumed digging.

⑨ Cross the road and look for the metal plaque by the right-hand window of Café Rouge.

This plaque remembers DJ Andy Crock, a stalwart of the legendary and cutting-edge Zap Club. In case you think you're being instructed by the sign to 'use your loaf', this was actually the name of a night at The Escape club, now called Patterns.

⑩ Continue past Café Rouge, take the first left into Nile Street and look for a new stone plaque on a column to your right – a touching memorial to a man 'who so loved the lanes'. At the end of Nile Street go left towards two pubs – The Cricketers and The Black Lion.

The upstairs bar in The Cricketers is the Greene Room, named after Graham Greene, a regular who is said to have written parts of Brighton Rock here. Another former guest was a man suspected of being Jack the Ripper. Memorabilia of both are in the Greene Room, which is only open on Friday and Saturday nights. If you want to have a gander (which we highly recommend) any other time you'll need to buy a drink, hope the pub's quiet and ask the staff very nicely if they'll escort you there. Next door, outside the Black Lion, is a plaque commemorating Deryk Carver, burned at the stake in Lewes in 1546 for being a Protestant, which gave rise to Lewes' notoriously extreme Bonfire Night celebrations. Carver had already established Brighton's first brewery, the Black Lion.

⑪ Go down the alleyway between the two pubs. At the end cross the road into a second alley, Ship Street Gardens. When you emerge onto Middle Street, there is a stone plaque opposite on number 20.

William Friese-Greene was an inventor of one of the first motion picture cameras and is here credited with 'experiments which led to a worldwide industry'. A slew of local inventors, chemists and photographers made Brighton and Hove the centre of the early UK film industry.

⑫ Walk towards the sea and turn right at the last turning before the seafront into South Street, unspoiled by progress, traffic or beauty. At the end, West Street, turn right to look

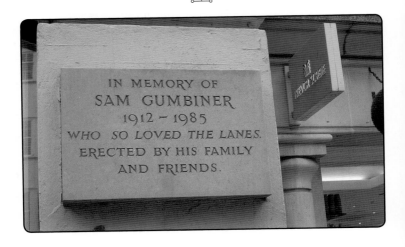

IN MEMORY OF
SAM GUMBINER
1912 – 1985
WHO SO LOVED THE LANES.
ERECTED BY HIS FAMILY
AND FRIENDS.

for a blue plaque on the third building on the right.

This is the site of the holiday home of Hester Thrale (diarist) and her MP husband Henry. Their friends Samuel Johnson and Fanny Burney often stayed here. Johnson was not a fan of the landscape of Brighton, writing, "The place is truly desolate and if one had a mind to hang oneself for desperation at being obliged to live there, it would be difficult to find a tree on which to fasten a rope." The only part of the house to survive is a garden post by the plaque, now used by visiting hen parties for 'scratching an itch'.

⑬ Cross West Street to the seafront road, keeping to the right hand pavement. After the cinema there is the large glass-fronted Brighton Centre. Go in the ticket office entrance at the far end, and if Holiday On Ice or the Jehovah's Witness Conference is on you should be able to get into the large foyer on the right and look for the Bing Crosby plaque.

Bing Crosby sang his last concert here in 1977, four days before dying on a Spanish golf course.

⑭ Continue next door to the Grand Hotel. Enter the hotel and go straight ahead to the impressive stairwell. Look for the brass plaque on the right hand wall.

This plaque remembers the IRA bomb during the 1984 Conservative Conference, which killed five people. Take the opportunity to nose around the building or take tea to the sound of the cocktail pianist.

⑮ Leave the hotel, not forgetting to tip your hat to the concierge, cross the seafront road to the promenade and turn right towards Hove. At Regency Square, as you cower beneath the dystopian shadow of the i360, look carefully for a small plaque on the lamppost marking the inauguration of

the first electric lights on the promenade.

⑯ Cross the road to the Melrose Restaurant and look for the severely corroded plaque on the left.

Continuing the early film pioneers theme, this plaque reads, "On this site stood the Pandora Gallery where films were first shown to the public outside London 25th March 1896."

⑰ Continue along the pavement until you reach the Holiday Inn, our final destination, and look for a shiny new blue plaque.

When the Bedford Hotel stood on this site, Charles Dickens was a frequent guest and wrote parts of Bleak House and Dombey and Son here. The latter even featured the Bedford in its pages, in the classic scene where old Mr Dombey complains to a receptionist about the WiFi charges on his bill.

⑱ From here you can enjoy the views of the West Pier from the bandstand, or stroll back to town along the beach, musing on the inscription that might end up on your own memorial plaque.

A wAlk oN the WiLD SidE

Combining a feast of activities with some downright silliness, this walk aims to celebrate some of the city's singular attractions and encourage those of an adventurous spirit to indulge in a spot of mischief and exhibitionism. While those familiar with the layout of the city are unlikely to be taken into uncharted territory, you will however be taking fairground rides, meeting spiritualists, beachcombing, winning prizes, hunting for Griff Rhys Jones and maybe even losing your pants.

Top tips: This walk should not be done alone or with prudish Aunt Doris but with a group of friends or a lover. To ensure everything's open it's best avoided during the winter months, and you'll want to set off no later than 1.30pm. If you're local bring evidence of your address to ensure you get free entry to Brighton Museum. Finally be aware that you will need cash for most of these larks so don't forget your gold lamé bumbag. And a wedge of Dundee cake.

 From the Clock Tower go down West Street to the seafront and turn left. The pier is 600 yards away

 1.5 miles/3-4 hours (allowing plenty of time for silly shenanigans and the odd pint)

 Begins at Brighton Pier (still called the Palace Pier by real Brightonians), finishes at Basketmakers pub, North Laine

 Pavement and pier boarding

 Police and security guards

 Getting chased, Benny Hill-style, by security guards and having a heart attack 37%

 Carry On At Your Convenience

There has been a ghost train on the pier since the 1940s and it featured in both Carry On At Your Convenience and Brighton Rock (though the interior scene was actually filmed in the studio). The original ghost train was a rare two-storey ride, until it burned down in a fire in the winter of 2003 and was finally replaced by the Horror Hotel.

② Head east to the other side of the pier to find the Dolphin Derby. This legendary game comes complete with its own catchy tune (which, if you worked here, would drive you to the point of insanity) and is a cross between skeeball and the Grand National. This is a full group activity which you must all keep playing until at least one of you has won an enormous cuddly sea creature.
Top tip: if it's not too busy you can cheat by stealing balls from the places next to yours.

① Our walk begins by Brighton's ghost train at the far end of the pier. We say ghost train but it's actually called 'Horror Hotel' and has a train running through it. Rather like a ghost train when you think about it. This is our first activity and requires a handful of tokens from a nearby machine or, if you're lucky, a lady in a wetsuit called Yvonne, who dives every few weeks for tokens dropped under the pier and sells them back to punters at half price. Draw straws for some brave soul to take the train alone and have a photo taken by one of the party at the end of the ride.

③ Your next port of call is the helter skelter, back on the other side of the pier and the epitome of old school seaside fun. Again it's short straw time as one of you is now required to descend its slippery, serpentine slope clutching the cuddly shark/ octopus/sea urchin that was won at the Derby and singing The Beatles' 'Helter Skelter'.
A photo is required as you hit the exit ramp.

Despite it being one of the ultimate symbols of Brighton (along with seagulls, drag queens and middle-aged men on skateboards), you'd be amazed how few residents have actually whizzed down the helter skelter. From the top on a clear day you can even see the Isle of Wight and Shoreham. Who needs the i360?

④ Walk back to the entrance of the pier, pausing for other photo opportunities at several of the head boards, which include 'Just Married' on the east pier side and 'Brighton Pier' in front of the main amusement arcade.

⑤ Leave the pier and find the steps on the left that take you directly underneath it. From here you will be heading west along the beach path (with the exception of following a slope up to the pavement and then down near the beginning to get around the café). Before that, however, you need to keep your eyes peeled for a tarot reader's room. One of you will now be required to cross his/her palm with silver, in order to discover what the gods have in store. If it's closed don't worry, there are another two on the stretch after the Seasick Doughnut. If they haven't predicted the winning lottery numbers and relocated to Hawaii, that is.

⑥ Keep along the beach path until you spot the giant orange lobster opposite the Fishing Museum. Stop here and photograph your cuddly sea creature with the lobster in whatever interlocking embrace you can muster on their behalf.

How rude this pose should be is of course entirely dependent on the marine species you have to work with. Once you're done, please post the photo to our site at www. facebook.com/CheekyGuides so we can be suitably appalled.

⑦ Head onto the beach now for a beachcomber-style scavenge. You are each required to find a stone with a hole all the way through it.

What you are searching for is a Hag Stone, also known as a Goddess or Druid Stone, and bringer of good luck. You won't need too much of it though, as our beaches are amongst the best in the country for finding

them – down near the waterline is the most fruitful area. Hag Stones are said to have many practical purposes: hang one on your bedpost to prevent a hag from riding your chest or put it in your stable to prevent horse theft by witches. If you're a resident of Brighton's gluten-free Hanover district, you'll probably prefer to use your Hag Stone as a toggle end for a bathroom light cord or an unusual earring.

⑧ Ok, it's time to leave the beach. Take the steps or slope just west of the beached wooden boats up to the promenade and cross King's Road where you'll see a few old school Brighton sweet shops. Each of you must go into Rock Shop and buy a stick of rock for someone you love who you've not seen for a long time and post it anonymously to them.

At the back of the shop they have rock imprinted with forenames, football teams and just plain rudery. You might like the tender

and touching 'My Nympho', or how about 'Lousy Lover' for an ex?

⑨ Continue east down the front, forking left of Queens Hotel and straight across East Street into an alleyway. A few yards down on the left you'll find the wonderful Mock Turtle tea room where you all need to chip in to buy one of their fantastic cannonball doughnuts. Resist nibbling on it for now.

The Mock Turtle was said to be the favourite tea room of legendary Scottish poet and comic Ivor Cutler who loved their cake and Welsh rarebit. If you've never heard any of his records it's your duty to purchase a copy of the apposite titled Jammy Smears, perhaps his finest hour.

⑩ Now head into and through the grim Pool Valley Bus Station keeping parallel with the sea until you reach the other side at the Steine (the fountain should be in view). The first person to spot Spider Cat up the side of Lace House here gets to scoff the doughnut.

⑪ Cross the road to Victoria Fountain, throw in a coin and make a wish.

Any pagans in your group will be interested to know that the stones around Victoria Fountain come from the same Welsh mountain range as Stonehenge. They were part of the broken remains of Goldstone Circle, a prehistoric monument that once stood in Brighton. The circle was toppled into a pit in the 19th century by a farmer fed up with all the visitors trampling his crops.

⑫ Cross westwards to North Street and take the fourth right down New Road, entering the Colonnade Bar next to the Theatre Royal for refreshments and a little dutch courage. The last one to find the photo of Griff Rhys Jones in here has to buy a round. Also, it's a double whammy for this unlucky member of your group - he/she is required to nip into the toilets and remove his/her

pants. They'll be needed for the next activity.

The publicity photos of thesps that have played the theatre next door haven't been updated since the 1980s, which lends the bar a pleasing time warp feel. Brownie points for anyone who can spot the odd two out, the owner of the bar and his mate (clue: one looks like a member of Abba).

⑬ Leave the Colonnade Bar, head left and almost immediately opposite you'll see the statue of Cheeky Chappie Max Miller. It's cameras at the ready everyone, as the pant-free member of your party has to get them hanging on Max's finger long enough for a photo. Be warned: security guards at the Dome may try and stop you if you stick around too long. If you do get caught and tortured, under no circumstances let on that we encouraged it or we'll get into trouble too.

The Max Miller statue suffers regular indignities. He's been seen wearing knitted ankle-warmers and even holding an electric kettle. It's what he would have wanted, we're sure.

⑭ Head away from New Road down the path by Max, hugging the walls of the Dome on your left. Follow the path to Brighton Museum for your next challenge. Enter the building and seek out the 'Images of Brighton' section on the ground floor where you'll find a flashy Lambretta in one corner. The tallest member of your group must clamber on for a photo opportunity, keeping an eye out for crabby museum staff as you do so. On your way out he/she must also drop a coin into Brummel, the fortune cat who sits near the gift shop.

⑮ Leave the museum, veer left and then left again as you head up Church Road past the Dome, Corn Exchange and Dockerills. Take the next right down Gardner Street. Half way down you'll find Cybercandy, who do a revolting range of real insects, scorpions and larvae encased in lollies. You must each buy one and post it anonymously to any seven-year-old boy you know.

⑯ Keep on to the end of Gardner Street, cross the road and continue down Kensington Gardens almost opposite. Half way down go in the little turnstile entrance of Snoopers Paradise. You've only got ten minutes in here, so set your watches and listen carefully. If you're a man you must have a photo taken of yourself wearing the most extravagant lady's hat or, if you're a lady, the biggest gentleman's overcoat. You must also buy a novelty gift (under ten quid) for someone in your party so decide in advance who's getting a present for who. Do not reveal your present yet.

⑰ Leave Snoopers Paradise, continue to the end of Kensington Gardens then immediately right down Gloucester Road until you reach the Basketmakers pub, our final destination. The person in your party with the largest feet must buy a round. The Basketmakers is unique in Brighton, and perhaps the world, in that its customers regularly leave bizarre messages in the variety of old tins that adorn the walls. Your final task is to each find a suitably fruity or funny message in one of the tins here and leave one yourself. Then settle back, drink in hand, and exchange your gifts from Snoopers. Feel free to spend the rest of the day or evening here, you've earned it! The grub is good too. Oh, and one last thing, it's probably time for your humiliated party to put their pants back on.

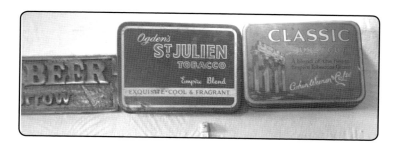

Ceci n'est pas une promenade artistique

Exhibit 13. Art Trail

For a town packed with 'creative types', Brighton's public art has always been something of an embarrassment. The seafront has a smattering of underwhelming sculptures, West Street has some cheap plastic illuminated cones and Churchill Square's concrete spheres are frequently mistaken for air conditioning units. True to character, Brighton's arty highlights have more organic roots. The city's biggest art hub, the Phoenix Gallery, started life as a squat, and the exhibition space Fabrica was created from an abandoned church. Taking you through the highs and lows of Brighton's creative expression, down graffiti-filled streets, mural-spattered tunnels and past outdoor sculptures, this walk finally deposits you at the Brighton Museum and Art Gallery for refreshments and the latest exhibition. Along the way you may even have the good fortune to meet local artist Chris MacDonald, peruse his collection of objets d'art and remind him that he needs to return our ladder.

Top tip: if you're a Brighton resident bring proof of address so you get into the museum for nothing.

 2 miles/2 hours (plus time for browsing gallery spaces)

 Begins at Brighton Station, finishes at Brighton Museum and Gallery (open Tues-Sun 10am-5pm, so time your walk well)

 Pavement all the way, spray-painted DMs optional

 The ridiculous to the sublime

 Being sprayed in the eyes by a graffiti artist 63%

 The Rebel

① From Brighton Station head down Trafalgar Street under the bridge, past the railway-themed artwork in the arches and go right into Frederick Place, pausing to observe the graffiti on the side of the pub.

The Prince Albert wall gathered street art for a while, until its virtually wholesale replacement with a commissioned mural of assorted rock icons. The only survivors are George Best and the kissing policemen, the latter of course by Banksy. At least, the original was. It's since been hacked off and sold into private hands, the current perspex shield protecting a mere facsimile. All this buggering about does throw into question the true ephemeral nature of street graffiti, leading one wag to inscribe "Poor Banksy, they put you in a frame." This, on the other hand, was quickly painted over.

② Hurry down Frederick Place (those of a sensitive artistic disposition should keep their eyes firmly shut) and turn left down Gloucester Road. After a few yards turn right into Foundry Street and find number 24. This is the abode of local artist Chris MacDonald. We are going to pay him a visit.

A retired teacher, Chris has spent the past twenty years in Brighton constructing beautiful and strange sculptures. There is something Daliesque about the way he juxtaposes curious metal gadgets such as old camera parts or giant cogs with beautifully carved wooden items, creating finished pieces that are wholly original: this is the work of a man who fell down Alice's rabbit hole and never returned. Knock on the door and, if you catch Chris at a

convenient time, he'll be happy to show you his work and even sell it if you cross his palm with silver. Speaking of which, please remind him that he owes us a fiver.

③ Retrace your steps slightly and continue down Gloucester Road until you reach Kensington Street which is fourth on your right. Here begins our graffiti tour which continues down Kensington Street and then doglegs across into Regent Street. At the end of Regent Street turn right then second left down Jew Street. Follow it around to the left down a short alleyway until you reappear in Bond Street and turn right towards North Street.

This graffiti trail features pop legends, superheroes, Brighton-themed murals and a multitude of bizarre images. Much of this stuff is officially sanctioned by the council in an attempt to divert artists' attention from other parts of the city. See if you can spot any decorated telephone exchange pavement boxes, which are part of a similar council project. Should you happen to run into a graffiti artist, a good way to impress them is to refer to their work as 'aerosol art'.

④ At the end of Bond Street cross the grisly North Street, watching out for kamikaze bus drivers, and head up the hill fifty yards or so to take a left down Ship Street. On the right hand corner where the road branches you'll find Fabrica, our next stop.

This former Regency church is now a gallery space that has exhibited some weird and wonderful installation art over the years, ranging from Brian Eno's 77 Million Paintings to a freshly-sown meadow. It's only open a few months of the year so don't be surprised if the door's locked.

⑤ Follow the road round to the right, keeping Fabrica on your right, then cross the road and head down Middle Street to the end, ready to make a mad dash over the busy King's Road. To minimise the risk of becoming roadkill, we recommend crossing where there's a small concrete central reservation just to your left. Once safely over the other side, lean over the railings and look to your right; it's time to experience your first official public sculpture.

Made from two tonnes of cast iron, this sculpture was commissioned by Brighton Council and bears the baffling name 'Passacaglia'. Its creator claims it was inspired by limestone terraces, shipwrecks and a lute solo on Sting's third solo album. While it may not lift your soul to the heavens, Passacaglia does come in handy if you want to try out a spot of parkour, or as somewhere for ankle-biters to play on.

⑥ From your vantage point head down to the beach and take the paved pathway eastwards, keeping your eyes peeled for a giant lobster. Despite any antipathy you may have felt towards the previous sculpture, it's worth remembering that in the backwaters of Australia and the US a giant plastic lobster still constitutes a major tourist attraction.

⑦ Just before you reach a ramp back up to street level you'll find the colourful Artist Quarter on your left, where we recommend a good twenty minute diversion.

This small stretch of the seafront is home to the workshops and galleries of a collection of local artists. These little rooms were once used for descaling fish but now sell art inspired by or made from driftwood, shells and other objets trouvé, together with handmade puppets and paintings.

⑧ Ascend the slope after the Artist Quarter and take a moment to view another couple of Brighton's public sculptures: the Kissing Wall and the Doughnut.

The blue slab of the Kissing Wall is a lovely celebration of age, equality and affection. You need to stand back a good few yards to be able to view it effectively. Down below at the end of the short jetty lies the Seasick Doughnut.

According to the Cheeky Guide to Brighton, its official title is 'Il Grande Bagel Verde' and it was donated by the Mayor of Naples in exchange for a large bronze herring. Other sources claim it to be "a speculative idea of what a black hole would look like", which is of course ridiculous.

⑨ Walk past the Palace Pier and take the steps down on the right immediately after it. There's a few small art studios here that are worth a quick browse. Proceed for 20 yards then turn left into a tunnel under the seafront road.

The slightly cheesy fairground-style depictions of musicians with Brighton connections in here should keep you guessing as to who exactly they're supposed to be. Zoe Ball may be speaking to her learned friends after seeing her depiction. Note that Leo Sayer has taken time out of his extraordinarily busy schedule to autograph his section.

⑩ At the end of the tunnel turn left and up the steps out of the Aquarium. Follow the pavement round to the left and carry on directly east. Pass the pillared colonnade on your left then cross the road to the seafront and you'll find Steve Ovett in front of you blocking the pavement.

For many years a bronze statue of the Olympic runner stood in Preston Park a mile or so distant where Steve used to train. That was until an enterprising scavenger sawed through his ankle and sold him for scrap. His foot remained, cemented to the ground and bemusing those passers by who had never seen the rest of him. This replacement statue is less impressionist in style and dare we say a little cartoonish.

⑪ Continue east for another hundred yards to a gated crossing over Volk's railway. Cross onto the beach where you will encounter the extraordinary Flint Grotto.

Created entirely by local fisherman Rory McCormack, this outsider art installation of bizarre stone figures is an unofficial but genuinely Brightonian work, and more in keeping with the spirit of the city than many of the officially sanctioned pieces.

⑫ Retrace your steps to the near end of the colonnade and ascend the ramp, double back on yourself past the giant copper letters that spell out I HAVE GREAT DESIRE MY DESIRE IS GREAT, and then hang a right up the next flight of stairs coming out on street level. Almost opposite you should spy a small square (more of an oblong really) called New Steine. Again, be careful crossing the main street here – there is a pedestrian crossing further down to your left – and head for the square.

At the far end of New Steine's garden is Tay, best viewed with the sea behind it. The city's newest sculpture, Tay is the UK's first memorial to AIDS and named after artist Romany Mark Bruce's friend, who died of the disease.

⑬ Head left down St James's Street. You are now arguably in the city's most bohemian street where many of the residents are themselves a work of art. Keep your eyes peeled for fruity Kemptown characters keeping the artistic spirit of the place alive, not to mention its off licenses.

⑭ At the bottom of St James's Street cross straight over, keeping Victoria Fountain on your left, and walk directly ahead. Head up North Street for 50 yards then veer right down the pedestrianised Pavilion Buildings. Follow the path that snakes around past the front of the Royal Pavilion towards Brighton Museum and Art Gallery, our final destination and home to a rather nice café.

In the museum keep your eyes peeled for the imitation Dali sofa, a plethora of chairs and plates and a modest collection of paintings and 'fashion through the ages'. Upstairs you'll also find the café and gallery area which often has some excellent exhibitions. And Eccles cakes.

SEX AND THE CITY

There's no shopping for Manolo Blahniks or supping on cocktails during this traipse round Brighton's landmarks of base animal urges. The city has its reputation to think of, after all. This is due in part to the Prince Regent, who built the Pavilion as a 'shag palace' and spearheaded the dirty weekender through his affair with Mrs Fitzherbert. More recent stimulation has come from the bush fumblings in the once-furtive gay scene, and Brighton's popularity with luvvies, their loose trousers and even looser morals. Whatever your lustful stripe you should find it on this tour of long-forgotten blue cinemas, cruising areas, sex shops, historical locations, ladies of the night, strip joints and hangouts that swing in a way that owes absolutely nothing to Charlie Parker. So don your dirty mac, stuff your pockets full of tissues and gird your rampant loins for a plunge into the steaming cesspit of depravity that is Brighton's sexual past and present.

 From the Clock Tower go up Queens Road (opposite West Street) and turn left 500 yards later where the road forks. Take the first right into Surrey Street

 4 miles/2 hours plus time for shopping, cruising and nudity

 Begins at Surrey Street, central Brighton, finishes Kemptown

 Pavement

 'Marital aids'

 Onset of madness from an incurable STI 18%

 Shortbus

① We start at the deep end with this walk. Surrey Street is home to two of Brighton's sex shops. It is your duty to visit both and buy a treat for your partner. If you're single, treat yourself. Having once witnessed a guy spend $10,000 dollars on sex toys in a sex shop in San Francisco with the parting line "I'm planning a night in by myself", we don't recommend wandering in with Granny's inheritance and a flaming libido.

At opposite ends of the spectrum, one is a typical old-school porn emporium, while the other (once voted best sex shop in the UK) has such a professional touch it makes buying a strap-on and gimp mask as unassuming as trying on a pair of Clarks shoes. Although the width-fitting process is slightly different.

② Head up Surrey Street towards Brighton Station, where countless furtive couples have alighted, signed in as Mr and Mrs Jones at a B&B and spent the weekend making the windows rattle. Just before the station turn left up Guildford Road to the T-junction which is Buckingham Road. Turn right and look for number 31 at the corner with West Hill Place, where a plaque commemorates the birthplace of one of Brighton's most famous residents, Aubrey Beardsley.

Beardsley was notable for his dark perverse images, daringly erotic for the time, which were famously used to illustrate Oscar Wilde's play Salome. Despite his being part of Wilde's gay clique, Beardsley's sexuality is unclear. He may have been bisexual and he may even have had an incestuous relationship with his sister Mabel, fathering the child she miscarried in 1892. He died tragically young of TB at the age of 25. In many ways he epitomises the town: young, arty, cliquey, libidinous... and a bit fucked up.

③ Go back down Buckingham Road, following it all the way to the end, and turn left at the T-junction down Dyke Road. At the next left cross into the churchyard, follow the path to the church and then right and downhill, where the path exits the churchyard in front of a large, grey semi-gothic structure called Wykeham Terrace.

A home for penitent prostitutes from 1850, Wykeham Terrace was also refuge for a girl accused of stuffing her baby down a toilet. She escaped conviction and worked there as a cleaner for the rest of her life, finally admitting the crime on her deathbed. The English acting institution Dame Flora Robson lived here in later life – fittingly enough, she played a prostitute on stage in 1931.

④ Continue down Dyke Road, past the Clock Tower and downhill along North Street.

Nestling comfortably amongst the high street shops on the right is one of Brighton's fully nude (that's the dancers, not the customers, so keep your mac on) lap dancing clubs. They also provide a bit of pole dancing, but sadly no ballroom.

⑤ Turn right into Ship Street and after 50 yards you will see directly ahead of you one of Brighton's more glamorous sex boutiques, owned and run exclusively by women.

⑥ Continue round to the left along Ship Street, then turn left down Prince Albert Street,

immediately passing the Friends Meeting House on your left where the local branch of Sex And Love Addicts Anonymous hold regular meetings. Follow the road along and downhill to where it meets East Street. Go right for 100 yards until you reach the left turning into Pool Valley by a pub.

Just beyond this turning is yet another lap dancing club. Note how these establishments are always painted black, the traditional colour of the stripping trade and chosen to reflect the type of hole they will leave in a punter's wallet.

⑦ Turn left down into Pool Valley and follow the curve of the road to the left and up onto the Old Steine through a gap in the buildings.

To your right, the other side of the the building that still bears the name of the Royal York Hotel, is the Royal Albion Hotel, that old rascal Oscar Wilde's favourite place to stay in Brighton, where he shacked up with his lover. Now a favourite with Brighton's stag and hen groups, its sheets are doubtless as sticky as ever. Go left to the YMCA (the letters marked high on the front of the building) on the corner of Steine Lane. Known also as Steine House, this was built by the Prince Regent to house Mrs Fitzherbert in a manner most convenient for him to nip over from the nearby Royal Pavilion for a bunk-up and a cigar. The building has been much altered since, but originally contained a massive central spiral staircase made of iron cast to look like bamboo, up which one Lord Barrymore rode a horse for a bet. As you do.

⑧ Turn around and, passing the fountain on your right, head directly east towards St James's Street (the main road heading into Kemptown) but take the small road to its right hand side, Steine Street, and look for a shuttered entrance at the next junction.

For many years this discreet club has played regular host to fetish swing parties that are open to all sexualities. Some people just go for the free condoms and lube. The charity shop next door now holds its annual sale of second hand fetish gear and equipment here, all donated by the pervy residents of Kemptown. Would you really want to wear someone's hand-me-down adult-sized nappy?

⑨ Turn left then right onto St James's Street and head east, keeping an eye open for saucy shops. Immediately after a large redbrick church on the left, turn right down Atlingworth Street and head for the seaward end.

In the days before speed dating, texting and nightclubs people had to flirt using a subtler method, namely the Sunday afternoon stroll. And where better than Brighton seafront where, if you were lucky, you might spot a pretty young lady, catch her eye, give her a wink the following week, greet her the next, then, after several hundred love letters and thousands of tedious hours sitting around in a draughty parlour making small talk with her parents you might finally get her alone and get to see her knees.

⑩ Turn left along the seafront and proceed for about 500 yards, pausing at the hedge-encircled Marine Square.

A basement flat here was the scene of a notorious murder in 1986 when the "granny

prostitute", 65-year-old Margaret Bolingbroke, was found stabbed to death. Matthew Richardson, the man convicted of killing her after failing to achieve an erection and being mocked for his flaccidity, managed to get the case retried, despite having initially confessed. Unfortunately for him he was found guilty a second time, and underwent hormone replacement treatment whilst staying at Her Majesty's pleasure and insisting on being known as Maxine Ryks. He was released from prison in 2013.

⑪ Continue east until you reach Eaton Place (look for the Hospital A&E sign), then cross to the seafront side of the road and go east a short way.

Down below is the banked off section of beach officially

designated for nudists, naturists and exhibitionists, and between that and you are the bushes officially designated for gay encounters of the physical kind. Access to the nudist beach is from the eastern end of Duke's Mound, the next right turning, where you can take the path through the bushes in either direction and find railway crossings at both the left and right ends of the beach. Decried by a town councillor at the time of opening in 1979 as "a flagrant exhibition of mammary glands", these days it flaunts more male organs than female, and possibly a number of fully clothed voyeurs. Which now includes you.

⑫ Recross Marine Parade, head up Eaton Place and take your first left into St George's Road. Turn right up Sudeley Place and left into Sudeley Street.

On this corner is the disused Continentale cinema, famed for the quality porn shown here from the 60s to the 80s. The consecrators of this former chapel might have taken a dim view had they known what was to come, but when closure threatened in 1986 Brighton's Argus newspaper made the wishes of the populace clear with the headline "Hands Off Our Sex Cinema!" The final double bill was a pairing of Off Duty Pleasures and Sexy Couriers. Porn titles were marginally more subtle in them days.

⑬ Continue down Sudeley Street. At this point the city's principal STI clinic is one block uphill to your right, so if the walk thus far has reminded you of anything you may want to get yourself checked. Go left down Paston Place to St George's Road. On the opposite corner is the teat-like dome of the Brighton Ballroom.

Prior to its various incarnations over the last few decades as music venue, ballroom and members' club, this building was a purpose-built mausoleum for the Sassoon family. Siegfried Sassoon had a complicated sexual life and an affair with leading light of the Bright Young Things, Stephen Tennant, lending unspoken additional meaning to his poem 'In The Pink'.

⑭ Go right down St George's Road, immediately passing St George's Church on your right, A hundred yards further on the left is our final destination and watering hole, the Barley Mow pub.

As well as serving decent nosh and old-fashioned sweets for sale behind the bar, the Barley Mow's unique Sperm Table ensures its place at the end of this walk. Turn left out of the pub to return to the centre of town, or you can catch a bus on the seafront road, Marine Parade. And for goodness' sake stop breathing so heavily.

41

A COUNTRY WALK IN THE CITY

Wild Park is often overlooked by Brighton residents and visitors as a place to walk and take in a bit of greenery, which is a pity. Despite being firmly embedded in the city, Wild Park is a designated nature reserve *and* officially part of the South Downs National Park. Coming here really can feel like you've just popped out to buy some shelving and a loaf of bread and accidentally discovered a secret escape hatch into the country. Be a little forgiving of the distant sound of traffic and occasional litter, and you'll find rich rewards: woodland trails, birds, butterflies, wild flowers, burial mounds, a dew pond and stunning views over the city and the sea. Within the first minute of this walk you're deep in the woods, so be ready to swap your stilettos and skinny jeans for a nice cagoule and pair of walking boots and you'll be just fine. Finally you'll return to civilisation with a nice cuppa and Marmite on toast at the park café, and wonder whether it was all just a dream.

 Bus 25 from Brighton Churchill Square or train to Moulsecoomb

 2.5 miles / 1.5 hours

 Wild Park, Lewes Road

 Car park to the left just inside entrance to Wild Park

 Up a big hill, along a bit, then down again

 Gigantic footprints, butterflies, lost dogs being herded by sheep

 Having your foot chewed off by a labyrinth spider 2%

 The Mosquito Coast

① The bus stops right by the park, shortly after the railway bridge. If alighting at Moulsecoomb station instead make your way down to Lewes Road and walk left for ten minutes. Enter the park by the main entrance off Lewes Road, where you see a deep tree-shrouded valley on the right. Take the driveway towards the pavilion café, ignore the first tarmac path with steps on the right, then after 100 yards head up the steps on your right. After another 30 yards veer left on the soil path and continue ascending, ignoring minor turn-offs. Not long after passing a few houses on the right, the path meanders up and down through the woods for a while, eventually bringing you out at the edge of an open field.

Wild Park was bought by Brighton Council in 1925, the date inscribed on the stone memorial that stands to the far left of the entrance. At the time of inauguration the area was practically treeless. The valley floor at the heart of the park has long had the moniker of The Giant's Foot, owing to the shape of the ground when seen from the top of the hill. It also bears the more sinister name of Moulsecoomb Pit and was the scene of two horrific child murders back in 1986. The dead girls were commemorated with a simple plaque on a bench and the

planting of two young trees by the pavilion café.

② Go into the field and turn left, uphill along the edge. Ignore all turnings until you're almost at the top and see a level sandy orange path, where you turn left back into the woods.

In recent years there has been some resistance to the erection of fences in this part of the woods, the clearing of scrubland and the introduction of sheep. The aim of all this activity is to protect the extremely rare habitat of ancient grassland, which constituted the bulk of the park until the late 20th century. Those who welcome the idea of sheep in the city centre can volunteer to be a part-time shepherd (or lookerer). All you have to do is check in for an hour or so a week to ensure they haven't been stolen by the

Hollingdean Ladies' Knitting Circle. To find out more, contact Brighton Council.

③ After around 250 yards turn right at a waymarked public footpath sign, passing through a gap in the trees and going right for a very short distance along the bottom edge of Hollingbury golf course, before rising briefly to join a track. Turn right down this track through the trees. This shortly leads to open land, where you turn left. A few yards ahead of you is Hollingbury Hill Fort. Follow the path anti-clockwise along the top of the fort's circular raised bank.

This area began life as a sacred Bronze Age burial site with four disk barrow burial mounds then, later, a hill fort. There is further evidence to suggest a building was erected here during Roman times, possibly a temple, though being Brighton it was more likely to have been a massage parlour. In the First World War the Hill Fort was used for trench-digging exercises. Its final humiliation was to become part of the golf course. Predictably there is very little to experience of the rich history of this site, except the circular shape and a few vague mounds. Nowadays those who get the biggest kicks out of the area are motorcyclists who like riding over the bumpy bits. And of course yourself, who will by now

be gasping with wonderment at the fantastic views of sea, Downs and dirty old Brighton.

④ After circling nearly 360 degrees round the fort, now with bushes instead of open golf course adjacent to the path, take a right just after a brick shelter partly visible in the bushes. Go left where you meet a gravel track then take the first right to rejoin the orange path where you left it earlier. Continue along this to the right as it shortly skirts the edge of the golf course then turns sharp left and descends directly into a big open meadow. This meadow is in the shape of a giant's claw, one pincer downhill below you and the other stretching out to your right. Note the pond off to your left. You now have a choice. Hug the trees to your right and follow the path for fifteen minutes all the way to the right hand end of the meadow and then back to the pond in a sausage-shaped loop. Or you could be a lazy git and skip to the next step.

This is stuffed in summer with skylarks, brimstone, peacock and adonis blue butterflies, green and great spotted woodpeckers and a host of wild flowers. Spring and summer bring dog violet, purple orchids and primrose. So try not to step on too many. Also worth looking for are labyrinth spiders who spin vortex-like webs on the ground and pull in their prey. Recent accounts of careless dog-walkers and their dogs being dragged into giant lairs, leaving no trace bar a set of dentures and an identity tag marked 'Trevor', are highly exaggerated. Labryinth spiders will never attack anything bigger than a chicken.

⑤ Approach the circular dew pond and take the path on the direct opposite side, which immediately heads right, downhill, through an elongated clearing.

The pond itself is a 17th century sheep irrigation mechanism. No wonder they get foot rot, standing in one of these things all day.

⑥ At the end of the clearing take the left hand path and descend through woodland. Keep descending diagonally, ignoring cross paths, until you emerge from the woodland opposite the pavilion café with the open space of the Giant's Foot to your left. You can easily find your way back to your start point from here.

You may prefer to explore the low-lying areas of the park, including a formal section to the left of the park entrance, nose around the monument at the bottom of the woods to your right or just flop out with a bacon sandwich and crossword in the pavilion café, open every day between 8.30 am and 2.30 pm.

Brighton's Back Passages

Ask any natives of Brighton for directions to Camden Terrace, Vine Place or Lewis's Buildings and most will shrug their shoulders, presuming you're mistaken, mad or, worse, got the town muddled up with Eastbourne. You'd have a right to sport a lofty air, however, as these are just some of the many overlooked alleyways and hidden corners that Brighton has in abundance. This twitten trail (twitten is a traditional local term for a narrow passage or sphincter) begins in a supermarket in the middle of town, winds its way to the edge of Hove, into the fringes of Seven Dials and ends back at the Pavilion. As we're attempting to cover virtually every twitten in the city centre be prepared for some grubby, dank alleyways as well as surprisingly stunning corridors filled with Mediterranean plants and art work. A final warning: some twittens are only wide enough to fit a single person so be ready for a few excuse me's and pulling in of stomach muscles when meeting a large, dark stranger coming the other way.

 From the Clock Tower go down North Street. At the bottom go straight across two main roads and enter St James's Street

 3.5 miles/2 hours

 Begins at Morrisons on St James's Street, Kemptown, finishes at the Royal Pavilion

 Paved surfaces

 Quaint little rear gardens, occasional glimpses of sky

 Alleyway walls closing in like the scene in the Death Star 0.6%

 Quadrophenia

① Make your way to Morrisons supermarket at 5 St James's Street. Go inside (yes, we're starting a walk in a supermarket, contain your excitement) and take the lift on your right up to the car park. Walk through the car park down the exit road and find a tunnel-shaped covered alley on the right. This brings you out onto George Street. Go right. Immediately before the Queens Arms hang a right into a tiny twitten that bends round in a U shape back to the same street.

The first of these alleys is among many to have been threatened with being gated off and thereafter inaccessible to the public. The second has in recent years contained both a Tardis front door and the Little Fridge Library, a refrigerator with actual library cards inserted into the borrowable books within. Don't you just love this town?

② Back on George Street, go right and then right again down St James's Street. At the traffic lights cross the street and make for the fountain to your left. Once there and facing the sea, head diagonally right, crossing the road, and make for a building with a frontage of black

mathematical tiles. Two buildings to the right is a three-storey brick building with red bands across it. Be bold! Approach the front down a slope, creep along the left hand edge of this, and enter the ancient twitten of Pool Passage.

③ Re-appearing at Pool Valley bus station, go right up the short pedestrianised street onto East Street. Cross it, head right and only a few yards away next to number 11 you will see a sign 'To Little East Street'.

This is the alleyway in Quadrophenia where Jimmy and Steph get it on and usually has a wealth of Mod-related graffiti by a doorway (though the owner does come and paint over it most days). Fans have been known to re-enact the love scene here.

If tempted, be aware that the chances of getting caught with your pants down are pretty high.

④ Emerge onto Little East Street, go straight over the road and up both sets of steps, continue across the left side of the square and enter the passage in the far left corner.

In the past this had movement-activated lights and ambient music installed in an attempt to calm passing drunken vandals. More recently it has been decorated by legendary Japanese street artist Lady Aiko.

⑤ Turn right up Black Lion Street and enter the twitten between the Cricketers and Black Lion pubs.

Along the seaward side of the alley are some listed 16th century cottages, probably the oldest houses in the town. The inveterate 18th century gambler Lord Barrymore lost a bet here when challenged to a race by the portly Mr Bullock, whose conditions were that he chose the course and be granted a ten yard start. Re-enact this event with a stout fellow walker and you'll find out why Mr Bullock didn't even have to break out of a slow trot.

⑥ Cross straight over the street at the end and dive into another alley, Ship Street Gardens. On exiting turn right onto Middle

Street and follow the road around to the right, past the Victory Pub. Turn left onto Ship Street and mere yards on, slip down Lewis's Buildings on your left. Look for the tunnel Duke's Passage branching off to the left, which logically enough brings you out onto Duke Street.

Still visible under brick paving or concrete is the location of the central gutter that used to carry noxious effluent down to the main road. Just beyond the Duke's Passage turning, look for the ancient swivelling iron frame nailed to the wall above your head. There used to be several of these frames containing mirrors that were used to direct daylight into the windows above, so that garment workers could see what the hell they were doing and avoid accidentally chopping off their arms in an automated mangle.

⑦ Head right up Duke Street, cross the road (West Street), enter the pedestrianised Cranbourne Street and go up the stairs into Churchill Square. Don't enter the arcade but continue on, keeping the mall shop fronts on your left, until you see a pub, the Prince of Wales, at the far end.

To avoid being seduced into a mad shopping spree keep looking to the right and you'll spot a pair of ghastly spherical sculptures. They are actually supposed to "sing" an

audio verite Brighton soundtrack with the volume turned up in proportion to the amount of sunlight. Stick your head next to one of the huge paddles, listen intently and you may, if lucky, just be able to catch the phrase "look, there's some berk with his head stuck to the sculpture".

⑧ Go through to the left of the pub and continue straight ahead into Clarence Square, then turn left downhill to Russell Square. Head diagonally to the bottom right corner of the square and a corridor with a pub called the Regency Tavern.

Pop in for refreshments at the Regency and a gander at its gaudy golden cherub-laced décor. In the 19th century this was known as The Gateway, because of a toll

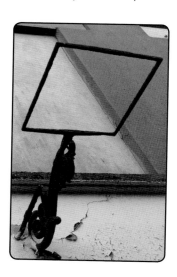

This twitten marks the boundary between Brighton and Hove. About a third of the way up look for a blue metal gate on the right. This is one of two spiritualist churches in Brighton, where clairvoyants ply their trade. Good to know if you need to find out where dear departed Uncle Roger buried the family treasure.

gate outside where travellers were charged a halfpenny to walk down the twitten.

⑨ On leaving the pub take a sharp left down Queensbury Mews and continue to number 1A on the right hand side.

Years ago this house was owned by a character called Tin Tin who became so incensed with the alleged nefarious antics next door that he climbed onto his roof and painted the words 'drug dealers'. The Queensbury Arms lays claim to being Brighton's smallest pub and, quite possibly, its hardest to find.

⑩ Turn right into Regency Square and cut across diagonally right to the top corner where a side road takes you into Preston Street. Go right up to Western Road and head west. After five hundred yards or so look for Norfolk Road on the right. Just after this, opposite the Duke of Norfolk pub, turn up Boundary Passage.

⑪ On exiting head right, continuing along Montpelier Place and Terrace, and turn left up Montpelier Villas, Brighton's answer to Sunset Boulevard. Turn right at the brick church, past Headroom barbers and go to the end of Victoria Road.

Have a look for the fake door painted opposite Headroom. The barbers was, bizarrely, turned into a bookies for the film Wimbledon and the painted door was a creation of the set that has never been removed.

⑫ Across the road opposite find the entrance to the twitten Vine Place.

The humble meet the well heeled here; to the right is the back of super-posh Clifton Terrace, while to the left are the small mill cottages built for workers at Vine's Mill, which stood just to the left of the alley.

⑬ On exiting, cross over Dyke Road and straight through a gate into the small park opposite.

Follow the asphalt path through here that descends into a cutting and deposits you onto Church Street. Go left and just after Kew Street, the fifth opening on the left, find the pleasant cut through called Crown Gardens.

The name arises from it being purpose built for employees at the Royal Pavilion and royal stables, back in the 1820s. The houses you can see by peering over the fences on the left look quite upmarket by modern standards.

⑮ At the far end carry straight on down North Gardens to where it meets Upper Gloucester Road and turn left. Cross the road after a few yards to enter Camden Terrace.

Perhaps the most beautiful of all Brighton's twittens, this is full of Mediterranean-style whitewashed houses and lush greenery.

⑯ Exit onto Guildford Road, turn left uphill and then right down Clifton Street. At the end turn right and then quickly right again into the charming twitten of Clifton Street Passage.

This is Brighton's longest alleyway, and still has some nice old street lamps and flint walls. You pass the ends of a few cul de sacs on the way which provide glimpses of the magnificent railway station roof.

⑰ At the end go left down the hill under the railway station

bridge past the Toy Museum, and take the third right into Trafalgar Terrace. On exiting, cross the street and head down Frederick Gardens by the Pond.

This twitten comes replete with gnome action at no. 27 and artwork.

⑱ On exiting take a left down North Road, then just before the Dorset pub go right down Orange Row, which eventually brings you out onto Tichborne Street where you turn left to meet Church Street.

More of a narrow street than a twitten, Orange Row is home to some of Brighton's most achingly hip live/work spaces. Obviously, they are numbered with fluorescent orange circular plastic discs.

⑲ Go left and then first right down the narrow bin-filled Jew Street, taking care to jump over any rats. This terminates in a small car park where you turn left into the newest alley on this walk, Bond Street Lane.

Created in 1981 by redevelopment of the buildings on the north side of Bond Street, this was inaccurately spelled as Bond Street Laine by the developers who forgot to check in their history books that 'laine' actually means field, hence the name of the North Laine district in which you now find yourself. The council occasionally erect a new street sign with the same wrong spelling. It would probably be easier just to rename it to something else. Maybe Bond Street Square, or Bond Street Plaza. Or Bond Street Street. La Place de la Rue Bond has a nice feel. Or how about Bondstrasse?

⑳ Hang a left down Bond Street to Church Street, where you turn right. Take the first right into New Road, then follow the pathway on the left by the Max Miller statue to your final destination: the Royal Pavilion.

The Pavilion used to run a 'Basement to Bottle' tour round the many rooms and secret passageways unseen by ordinary visitors. It would have made the perfect conclusion to this walk. Until such time as they get round to reinstating it, we recommend a nose around the nearby Brighton Museum and a big plate of Battenburg cake in their café.

A MATTER OF LIFE & DEA†H

Despite its rather unglamorous start on Lewes Road this walk covers some of the city's most tranquil corners, combining a solemn reflection on mortality with a celebration of nature's bounty. It serves, in fact, as testament to the creative and destructive powers of soil. In the first part you'll meander through the remarkable cluster of cemeteries and crematoria that lie between Lewes Road and Tenantry Down. After that the route ventures past allotments, the racecourse and more allotments, before depositing you outside an undertaker's in Kemptown. On the way you'll see some impressive monumental masonry, marvel at arboreal delights, march across a sacred Stone Age site and be treated to the best view in Brighton. Most importantly, there are some world-beating sheds.

Top tip: Cemeteries open at 9 am Monday to Saturday and 11 am on Sunday, while closing is 5.30 pm in the summer and 4 pm in winter. You wouldn't want to get locked in with all those Victorian ghosts; they don't half moan, mostly about how the country's gone to the dogs. Talking of dogs, they're not allowed in the cemeteries so you'll have to leave Bonzo at home.

 Bus 24, 25, or 49 from Churchill Square to Sainsbury's on Lewes Road. The cemetery is on the right side of the road just before it enters the one-way system by Sainsbury's. Use the stop before to avoid crossing a busy intersection

 3.5 miles/2.5 hours (longer if you linger in the cemeteries)

 Begins at Woodvale Cemetery, Lewes Road, finishes in Kemptown

 Risk of mud and a fair bit of clambering around

 Wheatears, Bauhaus sheds, Felicity Kendall look-alikes

 Falling asleep next to a grave and being mistakenly buried alive by Blind Barry the resident grave-digger 5%

 The Vanishing

① Walk through the gates signed Woodvale Crematorium and up the road. After a short distance you will pass the lodge. Take the narrow steps immediately after up to the left, signposted 'Pedestrian Entrance to the Extra-Mural Cemetery'. Go through the gate at the top of the stairs and follow the path down the other side where it meets a tarmac drive.

The Grade II listed Extra-Mural and Woodvale cemeteries sit cheek by jowl in this steep valley. In truth it's difficult to tell where one ends and the other starts but the impressive landscaping and greenery make for a pleasing whole. Note the dedicated picnic area directly opposite. For those who lean towards Gothic romance, this can be a good place to bring a loved one for a spot of lunch, quoting Keats and neck-nibbling.

② Turn right up the road towards a chapel. After twenty yards take the first track on the right. Ignore the next left whilst noting the curious Byzantine bronze-doored bunker on the corner and take the left after that. A few paces on this track bears right, but you go left by a tree and up across the grass, passing a mausoleum on your right surrounded by wrought iron flowers until you reach a tarmac track. Turn left.

This leads past an attractive array of catacombs on the right, and a gigantic sculpture-studded mausoleum just before the chapel. It belongs to the Ray family, and there's still room inside for another 28 of them. If one was a family member, we're not sure whether that thought would be comforting or chilling. Go right just before the chapel and round the back of it to be rewarded with the gravestone of Frank Laz Shoemaker, once a cavalryman for General Custer.

③ Immediately after the chapel turn right along the path signposted with yellow arrows. Keep following these arrows, which lead you upwards.

Try not to shiver as the path runs through a spooky overgrown wooded section of the cemetery, where abandoned tombstones bearing names of imperial adventurers such as Lieutenant Colonel Thomas Trusty Trickey poke crookedly from the undergrowth, Scooby Doo-style.

④ As the undergrowth thins out the graves become more orderly, and the path leads to a clearing where lies the austere but impressive family mausoleum of John Urpeth Rastrick.

One of the greatest railway engineers of the Victorian Age, Rastrick was chief engineer of

London, Brighton & South Coast Railways and responsible for the Ouse Valley and Brighton's London Road viaducts, and all those tunnels that make your ears pop. The mausoleum is built to resemble a train turntable, which is what they had to use before reverse gear was invented.

⑤ Keep following the yellow arrow-marked path, which rises slightly then turns right towards the road. At the road turn left and continue along until a yellow arrow directs you right through a gap in the bushes. The path then zigzags down the slope to the next road, bringing you out at John Ginnett's family grave, which is grandly topped with a statue of a horse petulantly stamping on the ex-circus proprietor's togs.

⑥ Leave the yellow arrow indicators and turn right down the driveway, and then shortly double back left up a cinder track that cuts up the bottom of the valley through a nicely overgrown cluster of some of the oldest memorials in the cemetery, along with some magnificent copper beech trees. You emerge onto a lawn, which you cross to find yourself in front of the crematorium.

Better viewed from outside than in, the crematorium was Sussex's first in 1930, and adapted from two pre-existing Victorian chapels. The section in the middle was originally a coach port, a sort of drive-through funeral area whose access road you've just walked up. The remnants of it still continue in a straight line out the back of the crematorium, as you'll soon see.

⑦ Go right across the face of the crematorium to find some steps that ascend next to a pond. At the top of these steps a clearing appears. Veer left and after a hundred yards follow the ground down as it slopes left to meet the old access driveway behind the crematorium. Cross this and continue straight up the other side, where the ground eventually levels out somewhat before meeting another driveway.

This corner, possibly the prettiest part of the cemetery, is one of toppled angel statues, sad disarmed shepherds and collapsed crosses, the graves dotted often haphazardly around the verdant hillside. So hilly is it, in fact, that you'll find the sides of some plots starting to crumble and wash down the slopes, so don't trip over any old bones.

⑧ Go right on the driveway which winds uphill to the Cemetery's Bear Road exit, jumping straight across the road into the City Cemetery. Take a right at the T-junction just inside the entrance, then first left, past the white First World War graves and their huge sword memorial. At a T-junction briefly enjoy the view of the Downs ahead of you before turning

right and heading up to another T-junction, ignoring a right turn as you go.

On the left behind relatively recent fences and gates, shuttered against casual visitors, are the Jewish cemeteries. Providing an intriguing lesson in the vagaries of stonecutter fashion, the more modern graves around you display a tendency towards devices such as heart-shaped stones, black marble and violet-coloured gravel. Beyond the graves directly ahead is a sweet little wildlife meadow, with a woodland burial area where you can wander amongst the recently planted saplings that serve instead of memorial stones for buried biodegradable coffins.

⑨ Turn right, and pause by the four-space car park to take in the spectacular panoramic view of Brighton. Rarely will you see more of the town in one single stare. Take the right turn here, watching out for the graves of German pilots shot down over Blighty in World War Two, then the next left and right to return to the cemetery exit.

Across the road right next to the Woodvale exit is Downs Crematorium, which offers a nice contrast to the cemeteries if you fancy a quick detour. The garden of remembrance, full of mementoes to the recently departed, is warm and touching. Among those remembered is

Brighton's most famous comic Max Miller, whose plaque reads, "I look for the resurrection of the dead, and the life of the world to come." It was the way he told them.

⑩ Climb up the main street (Bear Road) and after a short distance go right along Tenantry Down Road, which is surrounded on both sides by the lovely Tenantry Down allotments.

With luck (for want of a better word) you may be able to hear the whine of the crematorium in operation behind the allotments on the right. Is the proximity of those graves to the chirpy little carrots swelling under the surface a tad unsettling? We'll let you decide.

⑪ At the end of the road, where the fence stops on the left, cross over and walk up the bank towards Wyevale Garden Centre, crossing a second road on the way. Go past the garden centre and onto the short path, which leads into a pedestrian tunnel under Brighton Racecourse. After the tunnel turn right and follow the broad grass track, which runs parallel to the racecourse, in the direction of the TV mast. From here you have a fine view of the sea. As you approach the road you are close to the centre of the ancient site of Whitehawk Camp.

Believed to be 4,000 to 5,500 years old, Whitehawk Camp is the UK's largest example of a Neolithic causewayed camp. It's unusual in a range of features: the four concentric circular ditches, the four causeways intersecting them and its status as some kind of ceremonial site. Incredibly the council allowed parts of it to be built on, effectively interring

what had remained overground for so long. It's now a scheduled ancient monument, but despite its international importance you'd barely know it was there.

⑫ Cross the road and continue along the track path running parallel to the racecourse, towards the mast.

You're now on top of Whitehawk Hill, with Brighton spread out to the right, the Whitehawk Hill allotments on the left just past the mast, and beyond them Craven Vale. Both the latter have great open views towards the sea and some truly magnificent sheds.

⑬ Continue down the track. The life springing from the allotments on your left contrasts vigorously with the dead car seats and other flytipped detritus that often appear on the opposite track side. At the end of the track turn right just before Whitehawk Hill Road and descend with the fence on your left, until you come to a dirt crossroads and wooden waymark post. Head left and eventually you will pop out on Walpole Road. Follow the road right, past the posh school playing fields, and you'll find yourself on Eastern Road facing a sign for a Funeral Directors. This serves as a final reminder that, rather like a turnip, we are nurtured and dragged into the light, before being discarded in the nearest litter bin because we don't taste very nice.

⑭ Continue straight over the road, past the funeral parlour and you'll find yourself on St George's Road, where there's a generous choice of eateries should you want to stick around. For amazing coffee and breakfast we recommend Ground (to your left), for homemade lunches try the Hand In Hand pub (turn right and it's just after the next traffic lights) or, if it's some posh nosh you're after, treat yourself at the excellent Ginger Dog (back towards the funeral directors). To get back to the city centre catch a bus on Marine Parade on the seafront, where the nearest stop is a short way east opposite Seymour Street. Alternatively just follow St George's Road west as it becomes St James's Street and in fifteen minutes you'll find yourself back at the Old Steine, pondering the futility of existence, whether we live in a godless universe and wondering why these points never get raised on Gardeners' Question Time.

A VERY BRITISH WALK

What could be more British than a green and pleasant land punctuated by the sound of thumping hooves, caravan gas cookers stubbornly failing to ignite, balls being kicked and swiped at with sticks and posh young ladies learning to speak even posher than they already do? A celebration of all that is good and proper about Blighty, this surprisingly rural excursion round the eastern fringe of Brighton takes in a thousand-year-old village, a plethora of English sports, the grave of a Brighton legend, a majestic private girls' school, terrific sea views, fields of finches and wild fruit trees. Does it start outside a chip shop? Of course it does.

Bus 1 from Churchill Square to Whitehawk bus garage, get off outside Plaice 4 Fish, walk back past the bus garage and go east down the side of it (Henley Road)

5 miles/2.5 hours

East Brighton Park, sea end of Wilson Avenue

Small area inside park entrance or further along the driveway

Mostly grassland with a couple of short steep slopes

Windmills, golfers wearing colours they wouldn't be seen dead in anywhere else

Caught peering through school windows by matron 11%

The Belles of St Trinian's

① Find the entrance to East Brighton Park on the eastern side of Wilson Avenue directly opposite Henley Road. Follow the driveway, with football pitches to the right and tennis courts to the left, and turn right past the Pavilion café, housed in a nice old cricket pavilion that naturally enough overlooks a cricket pitch.

Cricket gets its first mention around the 16th century and is believed to have originally been played in Britain by shepherds, though their prototype knitted bats and balls were later replaced with the more acceptable wood and leather. By Tudor times cricket was as integral to the school syllabus as flogging, buggery and double Latin. It has always had close associations with Sussex, ever since the first recorded 'Great Match' was played here in 1697, followed a few years later by the first recorded cricket death, from a ball. It would, however, be a staggering 250 years before anyone had the sense to make the batsman wear a helmet.

② After a few more tennis courts on the left, go straight on up some steep steps in the bushes by a wooden sign for Sheepcote Valley. At the top of these, turn right and proceed for 50 yards or so until you meet a broad grassy track. Turn left away from the sea to eventually meet a wide sunken bridleway. You now just follow the bridleway directly inland. The right hand side of it gives better views but is closer to the golf course, so pick whichever side you like.

Down to your left you'll espy the Brighton Caravan Club site. A quintessentially British pastime, sitting in a metal box in a field as the rain lashes against the roof and an old episode of Minder chatters away through a snowstorm on a black and white telly, this is still regarded by some as the perfect way to spend a weekend. Whatever you think of caravans, they remain a valuable British asset – few things have the power to make Jeremy Clarkson so miserable.

③ Follow the path north, making for a small cluster of white houses ahead on the horizon. In front of the houses is a small car park, and in front of that is the white railing-lined Brighton racecourse.

While horse racing is of course popular the world over, the sight of faux-posh ladies in hats the size of a Ford Galaxy remains unique to Britain. Horse racing's relationship to England's archaic class system is, however, a complex one. Brighton racecourse itself was initially set up by the city's richest inhabitants in 1783 but by the 1930s had become a hangout for lowlife, razor gangs, ne'er do wells and accordion players. Nowadays, like most English racecourses, it is synonymous with touts sporting giant sideburns, men called Tony with fake tans and the aforementioned behatted women who only really come out to play once a year on 'Ladies Day'.

④ Cross the racecourse at the gap in the railings, go into the car park and turn right. Go through an odd U-shaped gate and onto a fenced track with the racecourse and then a golf course on your right.

As you descend towards the sea, a truly gorgeous view opens up of rolling downland framed by shimmering water and sky. This is an England as envisioned by Captain Mainwaring of Dad's Army, the "beautiful land" that the Germans "aren't going to get" provided of course that you ignore the post-war housing creeping over the hills on the left.

⑤ The path hits a dip and then starts to ascend. Thirty yards on take the right turning,which becomes a pair of multi-level tracks that curve back to your right, hugging the edge of the golf course. Keep on the upper left hand one. After fifty yards or so follow the fence left onto a grassy path that runs straight towards the sea. Keep straight for a quarter of a mile until the path turns sharp right around the field perimeter. Immediately before this take a path left over a stile, through some scrub and

directly east where the stately buildings of Roedean school for young gentleladies shelter behind the trees.

Roedean was founded in 1885 so blue-blooded young ladies could learn how to pronounce their p's and q's and hence bag a promising future prime minister for a husband. Eerily quiet, even on a school day, it boasts the longest school corridor in Europe (an eighth of a mile) and a secret tunnel that leads directly to the sea, where the girls can frolic in the water and dash back again without coming into contact with commoners. Famous pupils include Honeysuckle Weeks, Hermione Cockburn, Beatrix Ong and Zerbanoo Gifford. And no, we're not making these up. Roedean's most famous former pupil **is** *made up though: the lusty Lady Penelope from Thunderbirds.*

⑥ Keep the school on your right, going over first a step-through stile and then the more familiar type of stile, and turn immediately left inland, keeping the fence on your left. Climb the hill to the top corner of the field and go right, steeply down to a stile that lands you on top of a wall. Descend into the field on the left via a stone step and follow the path next to a churchyard wall on your right. Look for a stile on your right just after the church. Hop over.

Buried here in the graveyard of the 11th century St Wulfran's church (the oldest building within Brighton & Hove city limits) is Magnus Volk, part of that noble breed of Great British Inventors. Probably his loopiest invention was the colloquially named Daddy Long Legs, an electric seabed railway that from 1897 to 1901 ran along the coast here between Rottingdean and Brighton, the passengers riding above the waves in a little building attached to its wheels by seven metre long legs. Electricity and water of course make excellent bedfellows. Volk's plan to install hydraulic legs on Brighton's Palace Pier, so that it could be lowered to sea level to enable effortless paddling, went sadly unrealised. St Wulfran dedicated his life to converting pagans to Christianity. If he was alive today he'd no doubt have his hands full in Brighton and Lewes, where everyone seems to have converted back again.

⑦ Take a left down to the road, where you'll find yourself at the centre of the original village of Ovingdean.

With the exception of the modern housing cascading down the hill, Ovingdean village is a tiny haven of unspoiled English heritage, Over a thousand years old, it's the classic village of spanking squires, poachers and old Avengers episodes and comes complete with a large farm and beautifully preserved manor house. This is the moment when you must take out your water bottle (laced with gin) and drink a toast to Merrie England, its world-class feudal system and the good old days when you only had to take a bath once a year.

⑧ Facing the manor house of Ovingdean Grange, go left up the road and then straight on along a concrete drive where the road bends right. Continue straight, ignoring The Ridings' right turn. The drive becomes a chalky track that ascends gently, with horse paddocks to your right. You'll eventually arrive at the pair of multi-level tracks you already encountered earlier, so you fork left, and then a few yards later drop down to the lower track, this time on the right.

Keep your eyes peeled here during summer and autumn for apples and blackberries, ripe for scrumping, a uniquely British pastime as practised by Molesworth and characters from the Beano comic. While the strict definition of scrumping is to steal apples from someone's garden, of late it has also come to mean 'dry humping in public', but you'll have to visit Brighton beach instead to witness this.

⑨ Carry on as the path bends first right and then left   up the hill, following the track diagonally left across the golf course.

As we have discovered by now, nearly everything was invented in Britain, not least the fine sport of golf. Golf has been played in this fair land since the 1500s, though it wasn't until the 1970s, when such luminaries as Jimmy Tarbuck, Bruce Forsyth and Ronnie Corbett took up the sport, that the rest of the world sat up and really took notice. Notoriously sexist as golf clubs used to be, these days women are more than welcome, so long as they adhere to the strict dress code of fluorescent Pringle jumper and neatly trimmed moustache.

⑩ Cut across the trough of the bridleway and cross the first grass path downhill to the next one, which is the way you came before. Turn left and keep an eye out 100 yards later down to your right for a wooden seat that marks the start of the steps.

To round off our walk of all things British, what could be more fitting than a glimpse of the Union Flag which some patriotic soul has flying outside his mock-Spanish villa towards the seafront. You will need your trusty binoculars, but a good scan of the seaward rooftops should locate it. At this point in the journey it would be fitting to sing Land of Hope and Glory or, if you don't know the words, hum the theme tune to Rising Damp instead.

⑪ Head right to the steps, retrace your route to the park entrance and seek out the nearest chippy for an honest to goodness Pukka pie and a can of Fanta.

THE ALBION TRAIL

Pele, Maradona, Cruyff – the list of soccer legends who've never worn the blue and white jersey of Brighton & Hove Albion is endless. But, while the Seagulls' triumphs may have been sporadic, if silverware was awarded for wanderlust their trophy cabinet would rival those of Real Madrid and Bayern Munich. This path to sporting glory takes you to three of the club's four recent homes (the fourth one was in Kent, which is slightly too far to walk). Starting near the site of their old Goldstone Ground, it snakes through the suburbs to their temporary home in Withdean, then on through Brighton's northern extremities to the shiny new Falmer stadium. If you come out in a rash at the mere thought of football, there's plenty in this walk for the most ardent sport-hating, bandy-legged bookworm types. Despite a couple of brief but necessary trips through suburbia, most of this walk visits parkland, picturesque villages, some of Brighton's lesser-known urban green space and its National Lilac Collection.

 Train from Brighton Station to Hove Station, bus 7 from the Clock Tower or 21/21A from Churchill Square

 9 miles/4.5 hours

 Begins at Hove station, finishes at Falmer station

 Gentle slopes and one steep one, mud possible in places

 Away fans queuing at the wrong ground, lilacs

 Being roughed up by Crystal Palace fans 75%

 The Damned United

① Turn left out of the south side of Hove station and left again over the railway footbridge, noting the grand old perfume factory with its 'loveliness that lasts' sign. After the bridge walk up the road, go first left down New Town Road and second right up Goldstone Lane, which leads to Old Shoreham Road. Turn left along this, then cross the road via the central railing-clad island and enter Hove Park.

Behind you is Goldstone Retail Park, site of Albion's original home the Goldstone Ground. In 1979, thanks largely to permed scoring legend Peter Ward, the club hit the big time with promotion to Division One. The glory was brief and by 1995 they were struggling in the lowest league. Incredibly, the directors sold the ground to developers without having found an alternative home. The fans' indignity was regularly compounded by taunts about Brighton's gay population. Faced with the favourite Goldstone chant of "down with the Palace, you're going down with the Palace" (a reference to the hated Crystal Palace, sung to the tune of Guantanamera) away fans retorted "down on each other, you're going down on each other". To the left in the corner of the park is a 'heritage' board with more information about the old ground.

② Turn right along the southern edge of Hove Park, past the brick foundation stone, and follow the right hand path for half a mile past the fingerprint maze right up to the park's very top right corner. Cross to the opposite side of the mini roundabout and follow the Three Cornered Copse public bridleway, which soon enters a narrow wooded area, the largest in Hove actually. Where the path splits it's simplest to take the left hand fork, although any of the routes up will do. After about three quarters of a mile you reach Dyke Road.

In Hove Park you can spot wooden mushrooms, animal sculptures and a maze mapped around a fingerprint. Refreshments can be had at the top of Dyke Road in the Hill Top Café, beloved of van drivers and travelling salesmen.

③ Turn right down Dyke Road and 200 yards on take the second left down Valley Drive. The road soon bends sharply right and continues downhill. After about half a mile you'll find Withdean Stadium on your right. Follow the road round to the right as it hugs the stadium perimeter.

Valley Drive is just the sort of road in which footballers lived in the 70s. Listen carefully and you'll swear you can hear Brotherhood of Man drifting

out from Peter Ward's top-of-the-range Sanyo Music Centre. In those days footballers' wives were called Jean and worked in fashion boutiques, rather than owning them. By 1997 Ward was a distant memory. Following their last game at the Goldstone, Albion came within a whisker of relegation from the league. For the next two seasons the club shared Gillingham's ground, conveniently situated a mere 75 miles away, before transferring to the Withdean Stadium. The ground was not amongst the best in league football, lacking a roof, proper changing rooms and, most importantly, atmosphere.

④ Opposite the front of the stadium turn down Tongdean Lane under the railway bridge. Continue to the T-junction with London Road, cross over and go 30 yards left into Withdean Park. Head directly away from the road up through the park, towards a large gap between the bushes, and enter the park's fenced-off central section through a gate. Continue uphill, exiting via the top gate and going further uphill to the path which enters the wooded area slightly to your right. Stay on the main path, which veers left and shortly brings you out at a road.

The fenced-off section houses the National Lilac Collection. First planted in the 1960s, it features more than 320 types of lilac which are, curiously, from the same family as the olive. When the flowers are in full bloom in May and June it's quite spectacular. In 2009 the collection was temporarily decimated by professional thieves, who were thought to be selling the blooms to florists. In any other city they'd steal iPhones.

⑤ Go left along the road to a junction, where you turn left downhill along Braybon Avenue. At the bottom cross the road and continue along Warmdene Road. We would like to take this opportunity to apologise for this section, during which we recommend you pass the time by recalling the best Christmas presents you ever received, and the worst haircut. At the end of Warmdene Road, cross the road into Ladies Mile Close. After 50 yards you'll see a kids' play area. Turn sharp right onto the grass keeping the playground on your left and head up the path, which runs parallel to the trees.

This is a good spot to look back and enjoy the views of the edge of Brighton, the Downs, distant windmills and the sea of suburbia we're about to leave behind.

⑥ After passing in and out of the trees and bushes, the path eventually crosses another one and becomes the Ladies Mile nature reserve. Head up the hill and aim for the radio mast which will soon become visible. After half a mile pass by the mast and continue along

the right edge of the field for another few hundred yards until you reach the roundabout near the busy A27, via a small gap in the bushes.

⑦ Cross the road bridge over the dual carriageway and take the path uphill between the short wooden bollards on the far side of the next roundabout. After a few yards turn left through a gate and go diagonally up the field. At the top pass through another gate, cross the road and go up the path opposite, which leads to a small car park. Walk straight ahead through the car park and along the track opposite, which soon becomes a tarmac lane. Have a gander at the plethora of creatures attached to a house at the start of the lane. The Falmer stadium soon comes into view as this pretty byway

descends for a mile towards the charming village of Stanmer. At the T-junction turn right into the village.

Unless you brought a picnic you're probably famished by now. Stanmer Tea Rooms makes the perfect stopping point for some nice food and awful coffee.

⑧ Carry on past the tea rooms and at the T-junction turn left of the village church, going just past the pond. Go through a gate on your left, proceeding uphill through a field towards the large gap between wooded areas at the crest. At the top is a fence with another field beyond. Go through the wooden gate at the left end of this fence, and immediately right through a metal gate. Follow the line of a fence on your left straight downhill towards the left edge of the Sussex University campus.

⑨ Go through another gate on the left and continue downhill next to the campus buildings and through another gate into woodland. Turn immediately left along the fence for 50 yards, and then follow the path right and down to flat ground. Look for a green arrowed waymark US12 and follow it left as it winds steeply uphill through the woods.

⑩ As the path flattens out you'll ignore the first turnoff to the right and instead go left at the T-junction shortly after. After 30 yards take the path that goes right, doubling back slightly. Continue along this path for 15 minutes or so, crossing straight over a tarmac road and continuing through more woodland. The path ends at a road in the northern rump of Falmer village. Cross the road and go straight down Park Street towards the Swan Inn.

Former landlord John Woodruff was one of the new stadium's most vocal opponents and at one stage refused to serve customers who wouldn't sign his petition against the development. If you're an Albion fan it's now safe to go in as the the new owners are jolly welcoming.

⑪ Just past the pub take the footbridge right to the southern part of Falmer and follow the

street into the village centre, an idyllic spot save for the constant roar of traffic from the main road. Go clockwise round the pond, passing the church and farm entrance, then, ignoring the right turn back to the village, follow the lane straight to a crossroads. Cross over and along the road skirting the southern side of the Albion's new stadium.

Following an epic planning battle, the Falmer stadium plans were approved by the Government in 2007 and it was completed in time for the 2011/2012 season. It was named the American Express Community Stadium. Who says the game has lost all its romance? The impressive structure has 22,500 seats, around three times as many as Withdean, and finally provides a home commensurate with the team's current stature.

⑫ Once past the stadium, turn right to find the bus stop, or carry on past the campus of Brighton University, and follow the signs to Falmer rail station.

The Suicide Stroll

This attractive but sobering walk is a tribute to the stream-of-consciousness author and arch miserablist Virginia Woolf. Starting at Southease's brutalist railway station, it wanders into the village itself then loops around to Rodmell where it passes Virginia's former home, Monk's House. From there you trace her last walk, to the stark River Ouse, where in 1941 Woolf committed suicide. The circuit is completed with a tranquil amble along the riverbank, a particularly fine spot for birdlife. Since it's mainly on the flat this is a perfect, gentle, shake-off-the-hangover type of stroll. In winter, however, or on overcast and windy days it can be a tad oppressive. If attempted in conjunction with a relationship break-up, Joy Division on the headphones and the discovery of your first grey pube, you're advised to keep well away from the water's edge.

 Train from Brighton Station to Southease

 4 miles/2 hours

 Southease Station

 Approach Southease on the A26 and park on the verge opposite the turnoff for the station

 Flat apart from one short steep climb

 Merlin, egrets, short-eared owls, lesser spotted miserablists

 Deciding to read 'To The Lighthouse' and wasting eight hours of your life wading through molasses 15%

 The Hours

① At Southease station cross over the tracks via the pedestrian gates and walk down the lane a half mile or so to Southease village. The road takes you across the Ouse, with good views up and down the river.

Southease station is quite something. If you're hoping that it comes complete with a Café Nero, a WH Smith and a Tie Rack, think again. Indeed, if you're after a ticket office, a member of staff or a toilet, you're heading for real disappointment. Its only charm derives from the juxtaposition of its peaceful rural setting and an architectural style reminiscent of a 1960s Warsaw suburb.

② When you reach the village green, take the road that forks up to the right of the church.

St Peter's church, which overlooks the green, has an unusual round tower, one of only a handful in Sussex, and dates back to 1280. Beware marvelling at this sight while standing in the middle of the lane since it's rather popular with cyclists. One may come flying down the hill and leave you with a gear shifter permanently embedded in your navel.

③ Follow the lane up to the main road, turn right, then cross and go immediately into a lane and through the gate along the path marked South Downs Way.

After a short distance the path leads down into the bottom of the valley, taking a sharp right turn and passing through another gate on the way.

④ Turn left along the farm track that runs along the valley bottom. After about half a mile, shortly before reaching the farm buildings, follow the South Downs Way to the right. After the second of two gates it rises steeply to the right. As you reach the summit of the hill, head for the gate and 'To the Pub' sign.

⑤ Descend the tarmac lane for half a mile down into the centre of Rodmell. Just before you reach the main road, you will pass the old mill and a working forge. If you're lucky you might have the chance to stick your nose in and see it in action. As you reach the end of the road look left for the strange shrine, housed in the old petrol station kiosk, facing the Abergavenny Arms on the other side of the road.

Despite its modest proportions, Rodmell has a collection of fine old buildings and curios which include thatched cottages, a Queen Anne farmhouse and the Frank Dean Memorial Shrine. Former blacksmith Frank was clearly something of a local legend for his sayings, as they're pinned up inside the shrine and include such nuggets as "Well blow me down, I'll go to Peacehaven in a rowing boat." The Abergavenny Arms opposite is the only place to eat or drink on the walk. Luckily it's a rather charming country pub with a huge open fire, low beams and a reasonable menu with daily specials.

⑥ Cross the road and continue down the lane opposite. A few hundred yards down on the right is Virginia and her husband's former home, Monk's House. Although signposted on the main road, the house barely advertises its presence, so is quite easily missed.

The most dazzling of the Bloomsbury Group, Woolf was a central figure in the modernist vanguard, which overturned Victorian conventions and heralded the permissive society. Although best known for her experimental novels such as Mrs Dalloway, she was also an influential essayist, critic and feminist. In 1919 she

and husband Leonard moved to Monk's House and in her book-length essay, *A Room of One's Own*, Woolf famously wrote, "A woman must have money and a room of her own if she is to write fiction." JK Rowling must have missed this essential work. Although tenanted, Monk's House and its lovely garden are open to the public Wednesday to Saturday afternoons from April to October.

⑦ After Monk's House, continue down the lane, going straight on as the road becomes a bridleway. This leads out of the village into the water meadows and is soon bordered on the right by a drainage ditch. After half a mile the track brings you to the raised bank of the Ouse.

You have just retraced Virginia Woolf's last walk.

While deeply devoted to Leonard, in keeping with the Bloomsbury ethos of sexual liberation Woolf had a long and open affair with writer Vita Sackville-West. Neither this emotional freedom nor her professional achievements could rescue her from recurring depression. After her London home was destroyed in the Blitz, she could take no more. On March 28th 1941, in her last written words, she told Leonard, "I feel certain that I am going mad again. I feel we can't go through another of those terrible times. And I shan't recover this time. I begin to hear voices, and I can't concentrate. So I am doing what seems the best thing to do."

She then walked to the nearby Ouse, filled her coat pockets with stones and entered the water. On a more cheerful note, this section of the walk is a great spot for birdwatching. A keen eye (or expensive pair of binoculars) may spot a short-eared owl, merlin, buzzard or, failing that, a sodding pigeon.

⑧ Climb the riverbank and turn right. Keep on the path, which runs along the top of the bank all the way to the bridge, a distance of around a mile and a half. As you walk along the bank you get a fine view of the water meadows to the right, with their network of drainage ditches.

The Ouse is one of Sussex's major rivers. While the upper reaches meander through chocolate box surroundings, this lower tidal stretch has a compellingly bleak quality. The drainage ditches that run parallel to the bank are lined with reeds, whose feathery tops swish delightfully in the breeze and provide a home for reed warblers and buntings. The river is famous for its sea trout, which head upstream in May to their spawning grounds in the tributary system and are the heaviest of their species found in any English or Welsh river. Unfortunately, given the murkiness of the water you won't see a thing. Not a sausage. Or a fish.

⑨ At the bridge turn left along the lane and make your way back to Southease station for a final taste of post-war Soviet Bloc austerity.

Groovin'
in the
Ghost Village

This walk was designed by Brighton's inimitable musical duo Grasscut, as an accompaniment to their album *1 inch / 1/2 mile*. Since the music was conceived on the South Downs, this is the perfect environment in which to hear it. The journey descends through rolling downland and traverses the abandoned village of Balsdean, evacuated and destroyed by Canadian artillery training practice during World War Two. Of the farms, cottages, manor house and lunatic asylum, barely a trace remains. Only the site of the mediaeval chapel is marked by a lonely plaque. To do the walk you'll need the album, which is a highly accomplished musical romp through the Sussex landscape, incorporating electronica, dance, folk and classical, and peppered with spoken word pieces from the likes of Ezra Pound and W.G. Sebald. Even if it proves not to be your cup of tea, you have to admire its chutzpah.

 Bus 22A from Churchill Square to Bexhill Road, Sea View Way stop, 500 yards after the main Woodingdean crossroads

 4 miles/2 hours

 Woodingdean

 Small car park on the hill above Woodingdean at the junction of Bexhill Road and Falmer Road

 Easygoing bar one brief but steep climb

 Grasscut's *1 inch / 1/2 mile* – cheapest to get it direct from their label at http://ninjatune.net/artist/grasscut

 Frightened to death by ghosts of the old lunatic asylum 6.5%

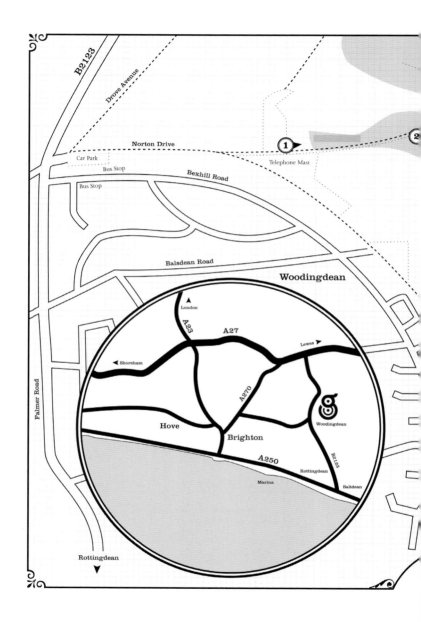

B2123

Drove Avenue

Norton Drive

Car Park

Bus Stop

Bus Stop

Bexhill Road

Balsdean Road

Woodingdean

Telephone Mast

① ②

Falmer Road

London

A23

A27

Shoreham

Lewes

A270

Hove

Woodingdean

Brighton

A250

B2123

Rottingdean

Marina

Saltdean

Rottingdean

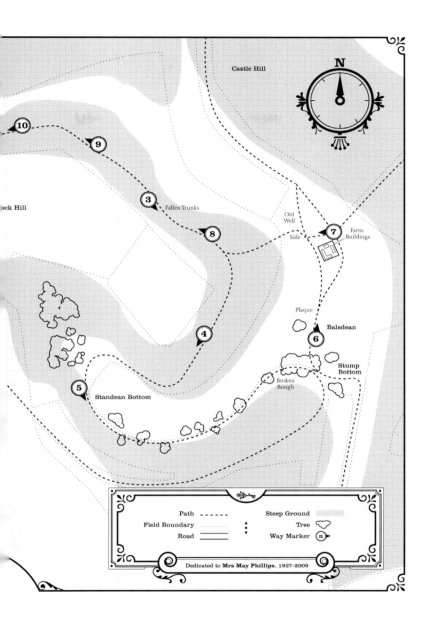

Castle Hill

N

⑩

⑨

ck Hill

③ Fallen Trunks

Old
Well

⑧

Stile

⑦ Farm
Buildings

Plaque

⑥ Balsdean

④

Stump
Bottom

Broken
Bough

⑤ Standean Bottom

Path — — —
Field Boundary ·········
Road

Steep Ground
Tree
Way Marker ⓝ

Dedicated to **Mrs May Phillips**, 1927-2009

If you've come by bus, go back along Bexhill Road to the main road and turn right up the hill. 50 yards later turn right into a dirt car park on the right. Walk over the bank on the left edge of the car park, and turn right along the track. Head towards the rightmost of two phone masts, beyond the houses. Two hundred yards before the phone mast, a path forks to the left by a fence. Follow this a short distance towards a wooden gate ahead.

① Begin track one, **High Down**, as you pass through the wooden gate, signposted 'South Downs Circular Walks'. Continue along the path ahead.

② As the path bends slightly to the right, there is an old gatepost in the fence, and a gorse bush with a concrete post in it to your left. Begin **Old Machines**. The path starts to descend into the valley and, to your left, the views open up towards Castle Hill.

③ The grassland opens as you descend out of the gorse and Balsdean's ruined farm buildings come into view below you to the left. The side of the valley falls more steeply and you pass the trunks of two fallen trees. A short way on at a third fallen trunk, begin **Meltwater**.

④ The path continues to bend right, and ahead you will see it disappear to the right where it rounds the shoulder of the hill. As soon as you spot this, begin **The Tin Man**, rounding the field edge down into Standean Bottom.

⑤ The path skirts the field edge and curves back to the left, towards a gate at the western end of Standean Bottom. Begin **Muppet** as you go through the gate, and follow the path past the hawthorns and into an avenue of trees.

⑥ At the junction of paths at the end of the avenue of trees, you are in what was once the centre of Balsdean. Turn left towards the ruined farm buildings and begin **1946**. After 100 yards, you pass half-buried foundations in a field to your right. After another 50 yards turn left off the path and walk up to a small heap of stones. Here you will find a plaque marking the site of the chapel.

⑦ Return to the path and continue to the farm buildings.

⑧ Follow the path to the right of the barns and go through the gate. Begin **The Door in the Wall.** Ignore the path ahead and go diagonally left, crossing the grassland uphill towards a stile a couple of hundred yards away. Climb the stile and follow the steep track back up the side of the valley.

⑨ Rejoin the main path, taking a moment to regain your breath. Turn right and start **Passing** as you retrace your steps towards the start of the walk.

⑩ As you ascend through the gorse land, begin the final track **In Her Pride**.

TRAINS N D BOATS N D PLANES

A wise man (oh all right, our friend Jeff) once said, "Brighton is like living in a swanky hotel. It's worth it if you're using the facilities, otherwise you might be better off somewhere cheaper and quieter up the coast." One contender is the little port of Shoreham, only thirteen minutes train ride from Brighton. Unlike its bigger and more slovenly siblings Worthing and Hastings, Shoreham has a charm that extends beyond shabby chic. Witness its clean, quiet beach, extraordinary houseboats and friendly, bohemian residents, all of whom are members of legendary folk group Crocheted Baguette. Making the most of Shoreham's proximity to disused rail tracks, water and the UK's oldest airport, this walk loops up and down the River Adur and Shoreham Harbour and is full of picturesque vistas and curiosities. On the way you'll be dive-bombed by private planes, follow abandoned railway lines, see a mind-boggling houseboat straight out of a Jules Verne book, have the opportunity to play Pooh Sticks on two different bridges and top it off with pie and chips at a classic pub.

 Train from Brighton Station to Shoreham Station

 4.5 miles/2.5 hours (excluding diversion to a 19th century fort)

 Shoreham Station

 Parking is available on the roads near the station

 Mostly hard surfaces, some grass

 Art boats, egrets, redshanks, herons, Hogwarts and a Cessna plane taking off with a trillion dollars' worth of gold bullion

 Joining a folk band 8%

 North by North West

① Exit Shoreham Station, turn left down Brunswick Road then second right down St Mary's Road, passing St Mary de Haura church. Follow Church Street as it bends around this lovely old building until you reach the High Street. Turn right and at the roundabout cross the road to the Ropetackle Centre. Taking the path by the left wall of the centre, enter the riverside walkway.

It's thought that Shoreham was first settled by the Saxons around the 6th century on a site half a mile north, now known as Old Shoreham. It wasn't until the Normans arrived in the 11th century that the current town centre area was settled. Today it draws the attention of mediaeval historians with the beautiful St Mary de Haura Church and Ye Olde B&Q superstore on the A259.

② Follow the walkway to the railway bridge and continue along the riverbank. The path soon meets a cycle route, which runs parallel to the path for about half a mile to Old Shoreham Bridge. You can usually take either route, although the lower path is sometimes submerged at high tide.

This cycle path is the route of the 19th century Horsham to Shoreham rail branch line. You can now cycle the route of the disused line all the way to Guildford, though lord knows why you'd want to go there. At the wooden bridge the old train tracks

suddenly appear, right where they once crossed the main road. Old Shoreham Bridge is an 18th century toll bridge and the only road connection between Brighton and Portsmouth until 1971. Now beautifully restored, it shows what can be done with a few bits of two-by-four. Incidentally, the Gothic-looking building you can see in the distance isn't Hogwarts but Lancing College, whose spooky crypt is open to the public.

③ Cross Old Shoreham Bridge and after 50 yards turn left along the riverside path, towards Shoreham Airport. The half-mile route back to the railway bridge takes you past some derelict wartime defences and the airport itself.

Built in 1910, this is the UK's oldest licensed airfield. Its magnificent 1936 Art Deco terminal is still in operation and houses a restaurant from which you can watch all the airport action. Not that you'll see much other than light aircraft, as the runway is too small for commercial airliners. Right here however is a good spot to stand and have your toupee ruffled by aircraft on their landing approach from the other side of the river — they zoom in surprisingly low and only just clear the fence.

④ Immediately after the railway bridge take the right-hand fork away from the river, following

THE DOME TRAINER

In the distance, to the right of the airport, keep your eyes peeled for the strange-looking green dome, built in 1941 by inventor Henry Stephen to train anti-aircraft gunners. Inside, footage of aircraft was projected onto its ceiling before an audience of trainee gunners. Imitation arsenal in hand, the gunners would shoot at the aircraft, triggering a realistic soundtrack of rapid fire, rather like a crude prototype of the Wii.

the 'Public Footpath' sign. This shortly takes you between a few trees and bushes to the edge of some open playing fields. A few yards on, the path briefly passes next to a narrow wooded area on the right, then veers right and continues along a low bank over a river inlet to the nearby main road. The path resumes across the road and follows the riverbank.

THE MASTER MARINER
HOUSEBOAT
MANUAL

NO. 72 THE PRIVY

NO. 9   HOBBIT GARDEN CENTRE

NO. 3 INVASION

NO. 53 CAPTAIN NEMO

NO. 15 SUBSIDENCE

Here you pass a collection of wonderfully ramshackle houseboats, which include a converted German minesweeper, Fische, and the eccentric Verda. Clearly designed by the Fabulous Furry Freak Brothers, Verda was constructed from the wings of a Red Arrow, an Isle of Wight Ferry and a 1970s coach. Nestled into its hull you can spot a car, a one-armed bandit and a wheel. Round the back sits a fire engine, serving as the owner's garden shed.

⑤ After about half a mile the path meets a road at the end of the houseboats. Cross the road and go down Weald Dyke till it meets another road. Cross to the beach and turn left along it for 20 minutes or so until you reach a gap between the houses, where a large metal corrugated-sided building can be seen ahead.

Shoreham Beach is a beautiful stretch of rare vegetated shingle, liberally studded with sea kale, yellow horned poppy and curled dock. Now a local nature reserve, it also provides wide stretches of golden sand at low tide. Planes from the airport sometimes cruise along here so be alert for any illegal imported contraband being surreptitiously dumped from on high for later collection.

⑥ **Optional diversion:** go all the way to the end of the beach to discover the remains

of a Napoleonic fort, now half sunk in the sands, built to keep those dastardly French ships out of what was then an important commercial harbour. Having paraded round the walls, return down the beach to the aforementioned gap.

⑦ Turn off the beach and go up Winterton Way, cross the road at the end and go left. Take the next right into Hancock Way and follow it to the waterside, where you follow the blue railings left. These lead you along the estuary edge, round a small mooring basin, back to the river and then finally away and back to the road.

There are always a few working craft of the Tommy Tugboat variety on this semi-industrial segment of the estuary, while the basin boasts a collection of yachts and motor boats.

⑧ Turn right and "enjoy" a brisk five minute walk along the somewhat bleak Riverside Road. Hang a right immediately after the Waterside pub and head for the pedestrian footbridge, which takes you back across the river to Shoreham High Street. Turn left for a selection of pubs.

The town has plenty of potential refreshment stops. The light and airy Crown & Anchor is an old pub that's been given the once over

by designers. Its floor-to-ceiling windows overlook the Adur and there's a nice riverside terrace. More upmarket still is Chambers Bistro, based in the old town hall building, a little further down the High Street. On the opposite side of the High Street is the true jewel in the crown, the tile-fronted Marlipins. A traditional, low-ceilinged pub with a courtyard garden, homemade steak and kidney pie at lunchtime and Thai food in the evening, along with a constant supply of Harvey's and Youngs ales. Sensibly, they don't sell Stella because, according to the landlady, "There's something in it that makes some people go a bit funny." They welcome dogs, heat their smokers and even throw in some free wifi. If you need an excuse to move to Shoreham, this pub is it.

⑨ And finally, for those who'd like to delve into local maritime history on a summer day that isn't Sunday or Monday, there's Marlipins Museum next to the eponymous pub. Return to the station by going back along the high street, going left into East Street and at the end right and then left up Tarmount Lane.

The Devil in Miss Price

This unique celebrity-themed walk is dedicated to local girl made good Katie Price, aka Jordan – model, children's author, novelist, businesswoman, philosopher and official face of Foxy Bingo 2007-2008. Taking in some of the most significant landmarks in Jordan's colourful life, the route visits the village in which she once lived, a beauty spot referenced in a lyric by spurned lover Peter Andre, an equine-powered well that inspired her range of children's books and a road where she was once caught for speeding. Even if you're not a Jordan fan the walk still has much to offer in the form of stunning views over Sussex, the beautiful Newtimber Hill, woodland paths and a hike through the centre of the mystical Devil's Dyke. And, given its eminently reasonable length, you should be home in plenty of time to curl up by the fire with a good book. One of Katie's innumerable novels perhaps?

 Bus 77 from Churchill Square, which follows Dyke Road all the way to Devil's Dyke

 5 miles/3 hours

 Devil's Dyke

 Car park at Devil's Dyke

 Hiking boots on for this one as there's a risk of mud and some knee-testing inclines

 A farm from the Domesday Book that's barely changed in 1,000 years

 Being run over by a pink horsebox 11%

 Real Life

① With your back to the Devil's Dyke pub, cross the public car park towards the brow of the hill. At the large stone seat, head half right down the hill. After 100 yards pass through a kissing gate. Turn right to follow the narrow but well-defined chalk path, which descends steadily across the steep hillside.

Our walk begins here courtesy of Peter Andre. During one of his countless reality TV appearances, Jordan's pint-sized jilted husband sang a song about her with the chorus, "Take a hike down to Devil's Dyke, you ain't worth shit – and maybe this song'll be a hit." Leonard Cohen eat your heart out.

② On each occasion that the path forks, keep left. Eventually it descends steeply down a flight of steps into the trees and through a kissing gate. Continue down the steps, then straight ahead for a few yards until the path meets a wire fence on the left, where it levels off and turns left towards Poynings. It leads between some gardens and then meets the main road where you turn right towards the more than serviceable Royal Oak pub.

For a while Jordan lived in Poynings in relative seclusion, in a fairly modest house near the crossroads. However, in 2002 a persistent fan tracked her down and began a campaign of harassment, sending her sexually explicit letters and

a pink thong. In response Jordan erected an eight foot high security gate, the posts of which featured two big shiny globes. The council took umbrage and ordered her to take it down, but by then she had decided to up sticks to a new house near Uckfield.

③ Continue past the pub then after 100 yards turn right to follow the path that runs along the left side of the lovely old petrol station and garage. On reaching a field, go over a stile and follow the trees on the left-hand edge until after 100 yards you cross the stile on the left. The path leads round a pond to the right and across another stile, past a wooded area. Where it joins another path turn right and stay on the main path for a couple of hundred yards. You soon reach a post, where a yellow arrow directs you left

uphill. This path shortly crosses a stile and continues climbing, opening into a field. Turn left along a grassy track. The grass track meets a narrow paved track where you turn right, and this rises to a road. Cross a stile and then the road.

④ Head down the track opposite. After 15 yards or so go through the gate on the left next to the National Trust sign for Newtimber Hill. Follow the path on the left that continues straight as a wide track over a small hump, ignoring two tracks to the right.

⑤ This section is about a mile. As the track peters out into narrow paths, follow the one that runs right around the side of the hill and gently upwards, with long fine views off to your left. Where the path forks go right to climb more steeply for a bit (over to your right should be a massive depression in the hillside), heading across the open hilltop directly towards a pair of distant trees standing in the open. At these trees, two paths cross – continue on the left hand one which crosses the undulating hilltop to a plateau and then curves around to the right. Keep going through scattered trees with dense wood on your left until you finally reach a small gate with a blue arrow. Go through it, ignoring the direction of the arrow.

⑥ Go directly ahead with two windmills at around 10 o'clock, heading slightly uphill between

gorse bushes dotted on the left and a line of gorse on the right. Keep on this path as it soon veers right around this line of gorse bushes. Continuing on the path, look to your left. The A23 will soon come into view, at which point you need to stop and take in this poignant vista.

It was on this stretch of road in December 2009 that Jordan was stopped by the police for speeding in her Jeep. A few months earlier, further up the M23 near Crawley, she was also done for speeding. On that occasion she was driving a motorised pink horsebox.

⑦ Continue to the long, long line of bushes and gorse and, keeping it on your left, follow it all the way to the end, ignoring a gate halfway along. At the next gate on your left turn right downhill. At the bottom of the field, the path plunges through a tunnel of trees and emerges through a gate into the hamlet of Saddlescombe. Turn immediately left over a stile with a sign to the Donkey Wheel. After 50 yards go right over another stile and downhill to the slate-roofed barn that contains the wheel.

Built to draw water from a freshly dug 150 foot well in the 13th century, the Donkey Wheel in all likelihood provided the inspiration for Jordan's children's book series, Katie Price's Perfect Ponies.

⑧ Go through the gate to the left of the wheel and turn right, following the left hand road past pigsties to a junction. Directly opposite in a small yard is the Hiker's Rest café.

Although only a caravan plonked in the farmyard, The Hiker's Rest offers a surprisingly good range of food. It's open every day from March to December, except Wednesdays. The farm is owned by the National Trust. As any Dan Brown fan will tell you, for a hundred years from 1225 it was home to the Knights Templar who were huge fans of the café's homemade pork pies.

⑨ Turn right out of the café and head back to the road. Cross the road, go over the same stile as before, but this time go immediately left for 50 yards, before turning right down a grassy track across the field. Go straight until you meet a stile, and go over it to find yourself in Devil's Dyke. You now have the choice of heading straight down the slope and walking left along the bottom of the valley, which involves a steep climb at the end, or taking the path immediately to the left, which climbs more gradually across the slope.

Popular myth has it that the dyke was dug by the devil in an attempt to create a trench to the sea, which would drown the many churches that lay in its path. His digging, however, was disturbed by an old woman who lit a candle, which caused a cockerel to crow, which fooled the devil into believing that morning was breaking, so causing him to scarper before the job was complete. On a different note entirely, see if you can spot the remains of the concrete platform where, in Victorian times, the UK's first cable car once launched people across the width of the valley to heady shrieks of excitement.

⑩ At the head of the valley turn right through a gate and head half right up to either of two gates. One brings you out onto a road where you turn right to get back to the car park, and the other takes you straight into the pub car park, from where you can catch the bus back to Brighton or treat yourself to some liquid refreshments at the Devil's Dyke pub.

Like so many wonderfully located pubs, The Devil's Dyke offers mass catering at the cost of rustic authenticity and intimacy. On a clear quiet day, though, there are worse places to sit than the outdoor tables. But wait a minute, who's that woman nursing a half of Guinness, sporting a black ponytail, pink leggings and face aglow with a veritable spectrum of bold cosmetic experiments? Surely, no, it couldn't be... is it... ?

WALKING WITH WEREWOLVES

Who doesn't enjoy a night time stroll? Anyone who's not a fox or a badger would be the obvious reply, but don't let your lack of fur or an extra pair of legs put you off trying this adventure into the darkness. A trustworthy torch or decent-sized moon will help stave off the jitters, and your reward will be an intense eerie silence not unlike that time Uncle Fred dropped his trousers at a christening. Beginning in the village of Firle, the route winds up onto the Downs, through clumps of moon-worshipping sheep and far beyond the twinkling lights of distant towns, before descending to the abandoned old coach road where highwaymen once plied their trade. The warm enveloping arms of the Ram Inn await you at the end with a decent pint and a jolly civilised menu. And if you haven't managed to starspot the Horse Nebula or Orion's Suspenders en route, blame the moon; sometimes it's so bright you can actually see where you're going.

You will need: Torch, water, phone, silver bullets, crucifix.

 Borrow a car for this one. Turn off the Lewes-Eastbourne A27 at the sign to Firle. Follow the lane to the left, not to the church

 5.5 miles/2.5 hours

 Firle, aka West Firle

 Car park on left on lane into Firle

 Up and down one big hill and the rest is flat. Risk of mud

 Owls, werewolves, witches, courting couples

 Walking partner transforming into a psychotic axe-wielding maniac who chops you up and feeds you to the sheep 6%

 An American Werewolf In London

① At the far end of the car park turn right, walk through the back door of the Ram Inn and then out again via another door in front of you. From the front of the pub follow the road straight on and then as it bends to the right pass the village shop and post office. Keep going over a small crossroads by some farm buildings. The tarmac runs out as the road becomes more of a track with wooden fencing to either side. There's a ditch to the right so don't go wandering off and break your leg.

② Continue on the track as it bends left with a high flint wall to your left and open fields on the right, climbing gently uphill. When you reach the brow, shortly after the flint wall ends, you'll come to a right turn, marked by a pair of trees standing alone with a double metal gate beyond. Go through the gate and take the chalky path that follows the right edge of a field gradually uphill, with a thick line of trees on your right.

The chalk in the path handily reflects the moonlight so this is an area where you can invoke some atmosphere by experimenting with a torchless procession and indulge in a spot of stargazing, now that you're well away from civilisation's light pollution. The first person to count 20,000 stars is the winner.

③ At the end of this path you'll come to a pair of gates, one metal and one wooden. Go through the wooden gate and walk uphill. After a few yards you'll meet a path that bends slightly to the left. As it winds up the hill stick to this path like glue; there's a sheer drop to the left which may not be apparent in the dark.

This is a steep climb so you may decide to stop and admire the view once or twice. On a clear night you'll see the bright lights of Lewes where another night of ritual pagan sacrifices is underway, while across the Ouse valley the shortest trains in the northern hemisphere tootle past.

④ When you get to the top of the hill, turn left and join the South Downs Way along the ridge. If it's clear and the moon's high enough look to your right for a glimpse of the sea. Keep going until you reach a wooden gate next to a gorse copse. On the left just before the gate are a pair of stony humps, which according to local myth are the remains of two fervent bishops who lost an argument with some witches. Go through the gate and continue on the hilltop path. It's pretty difficult to get lost here, but if you need a marker to follow, use the fence on the right hand side of the path as your guide.

A short distance on, you'll come to a small hillock next to a stone trig point. Here, sheep have been known to gather to sit and gaze at the rising moon. If you listen carefully you'll hear them grumbling to each other about how they can't get a wink of sleep with that light on.

⑤ Half a mile or so on, the path begins to slope more steeply downhill towards a wooden gate, followed soon afterwards by another. Go through both and immediately turn left through a rusty gate onto a tarmac road, with a small car park on your right. Ignore it and follow the winding road (Bopeep Lane) down the hill for half a mile, eventually passing a cottage on your left. Take the left turn onto a wide track very soon after, opposite Bopeep Farmhouse on your right.

You're now on the old Lewes to Alfriston coach road. As you stumble along keep an ear cocked for the phantom coach that rattles down here when unwary strangers walk in the wheel ruts, and for the click of the ghostly highwayman's musket as he demands 'your money or your life' and you try to explain that you've only got a credit card. More importantly, watch out for more modern forms of vehicular transport here too since the odd ratty Range Rover uses this track.

⑥ Keep going until you come to a cottage facing you at a fork in the road and follow the track as it bends around the left of the cottage. The track narrows here and if it's been raining this is likely to be the muddiest section of the walk.

This section of the coach road can be the darkest part of the walk, boxed in by trees and lurking menacingly in the shadow of the Downs. Naturally this makes it the perfect spot to hide, emit a terrible banshee-like wail and jump out in front of your fellow walkers.

⑦ Keep left and follow the track uphill. You'll pass the turning you took earlier in section 2 and then be retracing your steps back to the village, with the flint wall now on your right. Eventually you'll roll up at The Ram where warmth, succour and electrical lighting await you.

The ramshackle charm may now be missing from the labyrinthine interior of the last of Firle's original three coaching inns, but at least there's decent grub, since the new owners focus on local produce beautifully prepared. Keep a close eye on the pub dogs while you're stuffing your face in front of a roaring fire, though; their hackles always rise when they sense a werewolf nearby...

THE
LORD LUCAN
EXPERIENCE™

Let's be honest, for most Sussex people Newhaven is a handy place to catch a ferry to France and little else. The whole town feels abandoned, like a limbless toy discarded and left to rot in the attic, its stuffing long since eaten by rats. But don't let that put you off, it is precisely this theme of abandonment that offers rich bounty on our tour of the town where, in 1974, Lord Lucan's blood-stained car provided his final trace. During this figure of eight walk we'll take you to the area he was last seen and the stretch of sea in which he allegedly drowned. Along the way you'll encounter a host of other fascinating historical relics: the eerie deserted village of Tide Mills, two forsaken railway stations, an underground fort and a liberal serving of industrial decay. And while we can't guarantee this to be the most attractive walk in Sussex, there are still wide-open beaches, fine sea views and the chance to buy the finest fresh fish this side of Rick Stein's fridge.

 Rail service to Newhaven on the Seaford line. By car follow signs to Newhaven and Newhaven Harbour Station

 6 miles/3 hours (plus time to peruse Newhaven Fort)

 Newhaven Harbour Station

 The kerb on Transit Road, just off Beach Road

 One hill to climb, may be slippery on the way down

 Cormorant statues, fort, reed buntings, silver-haired moustachioed strangers

 Onset of depression from industrial desolation 14%

 Clue

THE
LUCAN
FILE
CONFIDENTIAL

With his cold beady eyes, brilliantined hair
and luxuriant moustache, Richard John Bingham,
7th Earl of Lucan, looked every inch the bounder.
Before his brief but spectacular criminal career,
the dapper former Guards officer was a first class
waster, whose Eton education had equipped him
only for the gaming tables of Mayfair, where his
success earned him the nickname Lucky. Rather less
lucky was his family's nanny Sandra Rivett, who
on November 8th 1974 was bludgeoned to death with
a lead pipe in the basement of the Lucans' London
home. His estranged wife was also attacked, but
managed to escape, telling the police it was
hubby wot done it. By then the cad had done a
runner. Three days later his borrowed Ford Corsair
was found abandoned in Newhaven. There were
bloodstains on the front seat and a length of lead
piping in the boot. Lucan was never heard from
again. Or was he? The day after the murder, his
close friend, casino owner John Aspinall — who
shared Lucan's extreme right-wing views -
organised a lunch for his friends to discuss how
they could help him when he reappeared. In all
probability Aspinall aided Lucan's escape and kept
in touch with him. Twenty-five years later, in
an apparent slip of the tongue while discussing
Lucan's disappearance, he told a TV interviewer,
"I'm more of a friend of his after that than I
was," quickly adding, "though I haven't seen him."

① Exit Newhaven Harbour station on the Seaford-bound platform side. Walk past the derelict station building, turn right and right again onto Beach Road. If driving, simply head down the side street and turn right along Beach Road. When it veers left, take the path that forks right and runs next to the wire fence. At this point you may be wondering about our sadistic tendencies. Don't worry, it gets better, ugly again for a bit, then much, much better.

The white canopied building to your right near the dockside is Newhaven Marine railway station. Remarkably it's the third one within a few hundred yards, marking what must be the highest concentration of stations anywhere in Britain. Although closed to passengers since 2006, Network Rail maintain the fiction that it remains open by running a daily 'ghost train' to Lewes which leaves at 20.15. Although the station is fenced off and passengers forbidden to board the train, Southern Railway will apparently provide a taxi service to anyone "in possession of a valid ticket". It is however impossible to buy a ticket.

② Soon after the path crosses a footbridge, turn right and over a bridge across a muddy creek. The path then goes left, before curving right, past some industrial units and onwards to the beach. To the right is Newhaven Pier, where two fishermen swear they both saw Lord Lucan walking on the morning after the murder. Turn left along the beach and you'll reach the abandoned village of Tide Mills.

Even without Tide Mills, the huge curving shingle beach makes this a remarkable location. The village was built in the 18th century to service the tide-powered grain mill after which it was named. It gained its own railway station in 1864 but a decade later was abandoned following severe storm floods. It remained intact until World War Two when it was used for artillery target practice but enough remains to give an impression of its past life. It would

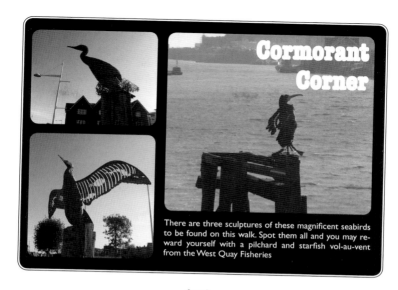

Cormorant Corner

There are three sculptures of these magnificent seabirds to be found on this walk. Spot them all and you may reward yourself with a pilchard and starfish vol-au-vent from the West Quay Fisheries

be a great spot to lie low if, to take a purely hypothetical example, you'd murdered your nanny.

③ Take the path that cuts inland through the village and crosses the railway line near the disused Tide Mills Station. Continue up the lane to the main road and follow the footpath left, parallel to the road. After a few hundred yards it veers left, shortly after which take the left fork and continue along the track, past the wooden bird viewing wall.

④ Almost immediately after the wall take the path that forks left. It soon enters a line of trees and continues along a raised bank for about half a mile. Ignore all turn offs and you'll eventually descend a few concrete steps. Continue next to a wire fence bordering an industrial site (this is the ugly bit mentioned earlier), then cross the edge of a car park, between two fences, before turning left to a road.

⑤ Walk to the T-junction and turn right past Newhaven Town station. At the next T-junction turn left and cross the railway line and the bridge across the river. Follow the road to the left then cross the road to your right at the second pelican crossing. On the other side on the left is Memorial Green.

The town council decided having war memorials dotted all over the place was too messy and confusing and so has gathered them all here. One of them has already been moved twice.

⑥ Go straight ahead down Bridge Street, then at the next T-junction turn left up the High Street. Shortly after the White Hart pub turn left down Meeching Road. This meets the busy one way system, where you cross over and turn right uphill. Ignore a back alley and take the next left, Norman Road.

Here, half way along outside number 26, Lucan abandoned the bloodstained Ford Corsair before joining Elvis and Shergar in the lost city of Atlantis. Either that or he still works at a nearby off licence, as some locals claim.

⑦ At the end of Norman Road turn left and take the next right, Hill Crest Road. After 150 yards turn left down a signposted footpath between buildings. Halfway down this path turn right before the fire station down the narrow Lorraine Road (named after the famous quiche), a mere track which runs between the backs of houses and soon has grass growing down its centre. At the end turn left down Geneva Road to a T-junction with Fort Road and turn right. Go past some playing fields and then turn right up the second of a pair of side roads,

Fort Rise. This brings you to the entrance to Newhaven Fort.

Newhaven Fort was built in the 19th century amid fears of an invasion by French market stall holders intent on selling pungent cheese and baguettes. Having seen service in both world wars, it fell into disrepair before restoration began in the 80s.

⑧ Follow the gravel path uphill to the right of the fort entrance, along the edge of a car park, and then left at the end of the car park. Fifty yards on leave the hard path and turn left through the bushes along a muddy path that emerges onto the cliffs at the top of Castle Hill.

You're now at the walk's most scenic spot, which on a clear day provides great sea views. According to Lucan's best friend John Aspinall this stretch of water was Lucan's likely last resting place. He claimed his friend probably sailed out in a boat that he kept at Newhaven and committed suicide by scuttling it.

⑨ Turn right and walk in front of the coastguard station and then some concrete defence remains. Just after these follow a grass path to the right which doubles back. After 20 yards go left down some steps through undergrowth, directly downhill for a bit and emerging into a car park. Turn right, and after 100

LAST PUBLIC
TOILETS
BEFORE
FRANCE

yards join an access road going left downhill. This meets Fort Road again, where you turn left.

⑩ Go right at the mini roundabout, down West Quay and follow the riverside path, which soon passes the fish quay, and eventually reaches West Quay Fisheries and The Ark pub.

Although primarily a wholesaler, West Quay Fisheries has a fantastic shop with fresh, locally landed fish at absurdly low prices. The Ark has a good view of the river. Food is lunchtimes only and is standard pub fare.

⑩ Continue along Riverside until you reach the river bridge, where you turn right and retrace your steps back to Newhaven Town Station. If you drove you need to return to your start point of Newhaven Harbour Station, but otherwise you're better off at the Town Station. Unless, that is, you care to take a second look at its odd stationmaster. You know the chap – grey brylcreemed hair, posh accent, hunted look in his eyes…

EARTH · WIND AND FIRE

Over two thousand years ago the Ancient Greeks believed that the universe consisted of five elemental forces, among them earth, wind and fire. Nowadays scientists scoff at such mystical hokum, insisting instead that 95% of the universe is made of dark matter. The only trouble is, they can't actually find it. Raising a goblet of dandelion and burdock to the more tangible symbolism of the Greeks, this simple but charming walk wanders to three extraordinary landmarks in East Sussex that are intimately connected with the names of the classical elements. Offering fine downland to stroll over, it incorporates a pair of windmills, a war memorial for Indian soldiers and a bizarre folly at the mouth of a railway tunnel that inspired a famous ghost story. All the more unusual is how each of these landmarks exists in relative isolation, hidden away amongst the hills, nooks and crannies of the Downs. There may be some of you who excitedly turned to this page in the hope of a route themed around the giant afros and eye-watering jumpsuits of the 1970s funk band, but then how you *dress* for this walk is of course entirely in your hands.

 Buses 17, 40 or 273 from Churchill Square, alight by the BP garage on the A273, walk back towards the garage and turn right and then right again by the pub, up the hill to the crossroads

 6 miles/3 hours

 Pyecombe village

 Parking on road just before crossroads by church

 Hills, grassland, muddy stretches, one winter quagmire

 Birds of prey, unusual buildings, Dickensian ghosts

 Being forced to wear a flour sack and perform The Windmill Dance 17%

 The Signalman (1976 BBC version with Denholm Elliott)

① Have a nose round the 12th century church to the left of the crossroads.

Pyecombe is an odd little place, sundered in two by a 17th century plague that saw most residents resettle half a mile away in what is now called Pyecombe Street. The old forge opposite the church was the source of the famous Pyecombe shepherd's crook, much coveted by bishops with a highly developed fashion sense. If you're not familiar with these crooks, check out the latch on the churchyard's rare centrally-pivoted Tapsel gate.

② With the churchyard gate on your right, go straight over the crossroads and coast down the hill (quack as you pass the mallard mailbox). At the bottom take care as you cross the racetrack they call the A273. Go ten yards to the right and

enter a bridleway through a gate, proceeding parallel with the road. After 100 yards this goes left away from the road and through a gate, up a gentle incline across open land.

③ Keep going straight along the fence line and into a wooded area via a gate. Watch out for a sudden clearing which turns out to be a golf course without any warning sign. Cross the fairway and continue along the path through scrub and woodland. A second golf course crossing has to be negotiated, after which you go through a gate into open country. Head straight across a couple of fields to the tree line in front of you and a barbed wire fence. Go through a gate and turn right with trees on your left and a hedge on the right.

④ After 150 yards the track turns left through a gate and goes up the right side of a field. Go through the first gate you come to on the right, next to a metal gate by a forest of waymarked blue arrows. Carry on down a broad chalky track towards the sea. As the track starts to descend you'll see the domed Chattri ahead to the left. Go through a gate and turn immediately left, entering the Chattri grounds 50 yards later via a gate on the left.

The fire element is represented by the Chattri, built almost a hundred years ago as a memorial to Sikh and Hindu soldiers from the First World War who died whilst hospitalised in Brighton Pavilion. It was here they were cremated and their ashes scattered at sea. The granite slabs on the eastern side of the monument mark the sites of the three original pyres.

⑤ Leave the Chattri, retracing your steps all the way to the metal gate with the multiplicity of blue arrows. Go straight ahead, following a vanishingly small track across open land, and then go through another gate. Keep going straight, following the fence line all the way up to the ridge and a line of scrubby bushes with a fence.

⑥ Go through a gate and turn left down a stony track with a fence on the left and a hedge on the right. The path goes through another gate and then gently downhill through gorse hawthorn and bramble. Fork right at a track junction. Just before a black windmill on your right, turn right along a path that skirts its perimeter. Follow the path downhill to emerge through a gate into a car park, and then left at the end of the car park into the grounds of a white windmill.

These two 19th century corn windmills (from the days when corn meant any old cereal, even Coco Pops) perfectly symbolise our second element, wind – though the cabbage soup at Divall's Cafe in Brighton is a close contender too. The first is called Jack, and served as the eponymous building in the Michael Caine thriller The Black Windmill where it comfortably outacted the rest of the cast. Though that one's a private residence, the white one, Jill, is open to visitors on bank holidays and Sundays, May to September. It's been beautifully restored by local windmill fanatics who are on hand during opening times to answer all your windmill-related questions. You'll get better answers if you don't address them as 'Windy Miller'.

1861, killing 23 and injuring close to 200. Despite an error by signalman Henry Killick being to blame, he was found not guilty by a jury since the poor man had been illegally forced to work a 24 hour shift. Dickens derived inspiration from all this for his ghost story The Signalman so naturally the tunnel keeper's cottage perched on top between the turrets is said to be haunted. You can even take tours of it.

⑦ Go back to the far end of the car park and through either of the two gates into the adjacent field. Go left down a steep hill, following the fence on the left as the path becomes a deep furrow. Go through a gate and turn left, still downhill to emerge by a lane. Cross the lane to a playing field, crossing this half left to a kissing gate to the right of a kids' play area. Once through the gate, cross the side road in front of you, and then carefully cross the main road. Turn right along the pavement and over the railway bridge. Peer over the wall at the startling portal to Clayton Tunnel.

This 19th century Gothic folly was built at the same time as the tunnel but its somewhat overstated nature remains mysterious. Burrowing into our earth element, Clayton Tunnel was the scene of a disastrous collision between two trains in

⑧ Immediately after the bridge turn left down a lane. After 200 yards go left down a bridleway, which is at first flat (and very sludgy in winter) before rising through the woods in a long gradual climb. Keep going straight on this path. At the top of the hill, traverse a path crossroads and go straight on until the path becomes a driveway and leads you back into Pyecombe.

The bus stop back into town is on the left hand side of the garage at the bottom of the hill ahead. Also down there is the Plough Inn, a strange conversion from Victorian coaching inn to wood-lined trattoria replete with chunky horse carvings and totemic wooden sheep heads. Their Italian cuisine is actually pretty good, and you can often just catch the strains of Boogie Wonderland drifting from the kitchen CD player.

CLIMB ONLY MOUNTAIN

Slide on your lederhosen and whip out your Alpine horn, because this energetic ramble takes you all the way up Sussex's very own Matterhorn, Mount Caburn. Oxygen, sherpas and intravenous Kendal Mint Cake can be arranged in advance, while those suffering frostbite or altitude sickness can bail out half way. Ok, truth be told it's not really a mountain – at under 500ft it's lower than most Brighton hairdos – but Sussex's stately peak would still have Heidi panting for breath. Climbing steeply from Lewes's base camp, the walk descends to a quiet valley before climbing again to the mountain's summit, where our Iron Age ancestors once strode. You then continue down to Glynde for tea or beer. En route you'll get gorgeous 360 degree views combined with ancient history and with any luck there'll be wildflowers, butterflies and skylarks perched on your shoulder. If you make it back to base camp intact, Lewes's Cliffe High Street has plenty of sources for rations. Don't let any frost bitten fingertips drop off onto your plate though – Sir Edmund Hillary did that once at a dinner party and someone mistook them for petit fours.

 Train from Brighton Station to Lewes

 7 miles circular (or 3.5 miles one way)/3.5 hours

 Lewes Station (or return to Lewes from Glynde Station)

 Mountfield Road carpark, just south of the station

 It's a pretty big hill

 Ravens, skylarks, paragliders and occasional glimpses of the Sussex Yeti

 Wind grabbing your anorak, turning you into a human hang-glider and depositing you in the English Channel 18%

 Touching the Void

① Turn right out of Lewes Station and take the first right at the Lansdown Pub, down Lansdown Place. Continue along the road (which shortly becomes Friar's Walk) for about a quarter of a mile, over a mini roundabout to the traffic lights. Turn right along the pedestrianised High Street, which after the bridge becomes Cliffe High Street.

To your right is the chalk cliff which lends its name to the Cliffe area of Lewes through which you're now passing. Cliffe Bonfire Society is perhaps the best known of Lewes's seven societies, partly because since the 1950s it has held its own Bonfire Night procession, refusing to join the main procession as that would require it to abandon its 'No Popery' banner. So, if you're Catholic and find yourself in the Cliffe area on November 5th, don't forget your rosary beads, you may need them.

② Continue to the end of the street, cross the road and up the narrow lane called Chapel Hill, which shortly rises steeply for about half a mile to Lewes Golf Club. At the end of the first section of the club's car park a public footpath sign directs you right towards a wooden gate. Pass through the gate and

continue straight ahead parallel to the fence, which will be to your left.

You are now in Southerham Nature Reserve, an unspoilt area of downland meadow. In spring and summer you'll be treated to a wonderful array of wildflowers and with any luck butterflies too. That's assuming that the thousands of skylarks haven't eaten them all.

③ Where the fence runs out after around 100 yards, continue straight ahead until you reach a wooden post. Take the right fork, which descends across the hillside, through a gate, to the valley bottom. Once there, head through another gate and past the man-made circular pond. The path heads straight down the valley bottom to the stile to the left of the Mount Caburn reserve sign. Cross the stile and turn right up the hill.

④ At the top go over a stile and turn right. You shortly meet a gate by another sign for the Mount Caburn Nature Reserve. Pass through it and walk the 100 yards or so to the Mount's summit, passing through another gate on the way.

Make sure you've glued your hat to your hair here as the updraught sweeping up the face of the hill can be phenomenal. Mount Caburn's summit contains the

remnants of an Iron Age hill fort dating back to around 400 BC. Reckoned to be one of Britain's most archaeologically excavated sites, it was found to contain over 140 burial pits, many containing artefacts as well as bones. The pronounced ditch and bank fortifications probably date from the later Romano-British or Saxon periods. The Iron Age tradition of paragliding survives to this day; during good weather the sky is thick with them.

⑤ Head back along the path to the start of section 4, but don't cross back over the stile. Keep it to your left and take the path right to Glynde, which descends for about three quarters of a mile, across three fields. When you join the road turn left. You can either stop at the Little Cottage Tearoom, or walk to

the T-junction and turn right to the station and the Trevor Arms.

NB. *If you can't face the walk back to Lewes from here after stuffing yourself with beer, pie and jam roly poly, you can catch the train. The Little Cottage Tearoom serves light meals, cream teas and cakes, and has a sweet garden. It's generally open on Fridays, Saturdays and Sundays from spring through to autumn. If you fancy alcohol or a larger meal, head for the Trevor Arms, which lies just past the station. It's a no-frills local with a beer garden the size of Belgium, but without the carpet factories. As you walk towards the pub take a look at* Glynde Forge, the wonderful old village blacksmiths on the right with its horseshoe-shaped beam. If you fancy giving it a try, owner Terry Tyhurst runs weekend workshops.

⑥ Climb back up the hill to the start of section 4 again, and, without crossing that stile, turn right along the high ground next to the fence and after a few hundred yards go over a stile. After about half a mile it becomes a chalk track, soon after which it passes through a gate and stile towards a dip. A few yards past the stile fork left down the dip, cross a chalk track and continue up the other side, putting increasing distance between yourself and the trees to your right. The path rises gently then gradually descends. Before long you reach a wooden post where you turn left and head towards a nearby kissing gate.

⑦ After going through the gate continue along the path, which heads gently down the field. It passes through a gate and continues its descent, eventually meeting the wooden post that you encountered in section 3.

⑧ From here you can retrace your steps to the golf course, down Chapel Hill, along Cliffe High Street, Friar's Walk and Lansdown Place to Lewes station.

Cliffe High Street has plenty of good eateries. At the bridge end is Flint Owl Bakery, which does some cracking quiches, salads and cakes along with its own artisan bread products. If you fancy a more restauranty menu then the nearby Le Magasin is your best bet. For pub food, try the John Harvey Tavern right by the river on Bear Yard, which has every draught and bottled beer produced by the estimable local Harvey's Brewery. Or if you want to find out how drinkers survived the 1970s, get into The Gardener's Arms for a pork pie and a pickled egg.

BUNGALOWLAND

Perched defiantly above the English Channel, Peacehaven is Brighton's strange little hillbilly cousin. Like a flatulent bulldog or Keith Harris and Orville, it has a singularly British charm. Our route brings you up close and personal with this bungalow wilderness and is one for those who fancy something a little different. What this walk lacks in bucolic charm it makes up for with rural noir, taking you to places you probably never knew existed and perhaps some you'd rather didn't. Starting with a suburban cliff-top saunter, it cuts inland and skirts the town's faintly creepy hinterland before leading you into the beautiful village of Telscombe and across its historic common, the Tye. On the way you'll get fine sea views, manmade eyesores and an awful lot of bungalows.

Top tip: there's no refreshment stops until the very end, so don't forget to pack a couple of macaroons and a bottle of eggnog to keep you going.

 Bus 12, 12A, 14, 14A, 14B or 14C from Churchill Square to the Smugglers Rest pub just before Telscombe Cliffs

 7.5 miles/3.5 hours

 Telscombe Cliffs

 Pub car park

 Flat with some gentle inclines, patches of dense gorse

 Kittiwakes, Belgium and weird shit

 Uncontrollable desire to buy a static caravan on the edge of rapidly disappearing cliffs 3%

 Deliverance

SPOTTERS' GUIDE TO THE BUNGALOWS OF PEACEHAVEN

One of the UK's original new towns, Peacehaven was founded during the First World War by entrepreneur Charles Neville. It achieved fame through a Daily Express competition to find a name. The winner, New Anzac on Sea, lasted less than a year before Neville changed it to Peacehaven, memories of the war's disastrous Gallipoli campaign not proving to be a selling point. Runners up in the competition were offered free plots of land, only to discover that they were charged a large conveyancing fee. This outraged the Express which sued Neville, but the publicity generated only brought more people to the town. The pioneering spirit that was necessary to build a home in virgin territory with no services whatsoever lives on in the idiosyncratic additions to the original bungalows. Here are our favourites.

BIG DADDY 6 points
Classic vertical development of an original single storey bungalow, complete with its own rooftop wrestling ring.

JOHN CAGE COTTAGE 4 points
Minimalism seldom comes applied with such purity as this perfectly symmetrical single windowed building that boldly mixes an arched opening with rectangular french windows.

LOFT A LA MODE 8 points
Inspired by Le Corbusier and Walsall Retail Park, this melds brutalist stylings with a nascent clifftop paddling pool.

RUBIK'S MANSION 7 points
Breaking all the bungalow rules by having multiple storeys, Rubik's Mansion is said to be owned by... yes! The man himself! The very man! None other than, erm, local plumber Ted Smith.

① Head towards the cliff edge to the left of the apostrophe-free Smugglers Rest pub and follow the coastal path east. Continue between houses and cliff edge for around two miles, passing first Telscombe Cliffs and then Peacehaven. Keep a look out for the King George V monument that marks where the Greenwich Meridian Line leaves Britain. It used to leave it 50 feet further south until they moved the monument in 1960, which gives you a good idea of how much larger the country was before erosion was invented.

② At the far end of Peacehaven the houses run out. The path continues close to the cliff edge. There is no longer a fence between the path and the cliff, but don't be tempted to go near the edge, as the ground regularly crumbles. You will shortly see a caravan park over to your left. Just after you pass it, take the track to your left, which runs up the side of the caravan park. Head to the top of the track then turn right and first left.

There's something rather unsettling about this area: the unmade streets, unfinished houses and fields littered with ramshackle sheds and disused vehicles. Filmmakers have exploited its noir quality. At the

top of the track, the white house you see to your left featured as a murder scene in the gritty 1962 crime movie Jigsaw, while back at the cliffs Jimmy comes close to suicide in Quadrophenia.

③ Follow the track down to the main road and cross over. It's a bit hairy here at times so be careful. Continue along the road opposite, Links Avenue, which is also unmade. Where it runs out, continue straight ahead along the footpath, which is fenced on both sides and soon enters an area of high bushes.

④ Where the path opens out into a clearing, ignore the signed path to the right (or continuing straight ahead) and instead go sharp left. The path initially doubles back, then curves through the bushes down the hill. At the next clearing go left again and follow the path until it emerges into a field. Keep on straight ahead up the right side of the field. The path eventually levels off and continues on the flat for around a quarter of a mile. On the left you'll notice a grass-covered industrial development.

Protesters began to refer to their own town as Poohaven when attempting to stop the development of this glittering new sewage works. If you feel any vibrations whilst strolling around this bit, the source isn't a ley line connecting your spirit to Gaia; it's the little trains they've got shifting waste around in newly-dug underground tunnels.

⑤ Soon after the treatment works (trust us, it does get nicer after this bit), the path meets a track, where you turn right. Where it meets a T-junction, head right and follow this road as it curves left. Skirt round to the left of a farm and continue on over a stile until the road starts to bend to the right, at which point follow the footpath sign over a stile directly left. This path brings you to a lane, where you turn right and head down the hill.

⑥ At the bottom, by the house with the pool, take the lane that doubles back to the left and heads along the valley bottom, rising steadily. After a while you reach a crossroads, where you turn right along the concrete road that leads uphill, and at the top of the hill turn left.

Again, this whole area feels rather off-centre and more like a frontier outpost than a town on an overdeveloped coastline.

⑦ Keep on along this unmade road until it veers left, then follow the public bridleway that goes straight on, which shortly brings you to the church in the lovely village of Telscombe.

The village dates back to before the Domesday Book. Its main claim to fame is that in 1902 the Lord of the Manor, Ambrose Gorham, won the Grand National on his horse Shannon Lass. He spent his winnings on bringing water and electricity to the village. Strangely for one involved in horse racing, Ambrose insisted that no pubs should be allowed in the village. Its location at the end of a two-mile dead end road lends the place an almost unearthly serenity. Turn right here if you'd like to have a nose about, and then return to this spot.

⑧ Turn left at the church and walk up the hill, past the youth hostel. At the top of the hill, you reach the area known as Telscombe Tye, where the road runs out. Take the main track that carries straight on from the road, as opposed to the one that heads down the left-hand side.

The Tye is a lovely stretch of ancient common land, which divides Telscombe from Telscombe Cliffs. Although the two communities lie less than a mile apart, the road connecting the two is over eight miles. The conceptual journey, however, is even greater, as the two places are as different as chalk and Thursdays. As well as being a haven for wildflowers, insects and ground nesting birds, the Tye's North West corner is home to a small Bronze Age barrow.

⑨ After about a mile, veer left across the grass so that you descend to the bottom left corner of the common, where there's a gate through to the main road and a handy pedestrian crossing. Cross the road to The Smugglers Rest. A hundred yards or so down from the pub you can take a bus back to Brighton.

Previously the faux rustic Badgers Watch, the faux rustic The Smugglers Rest may lack atmosphere but is worth a visit for the wonderful sea views from its rear terrace. For a less corporate experience without the occasional whiff of wastewater treatment try the Telscombe Tavern a few hundred yards east.

BOTTOMS UP!

"Everything's bottoms with you people, isn't it?" sneered Basil Fawlty at the brash American in Fawlty Towers. The truth of course is that it is the English who have a far greater obsession with posteriors, particularly those belonging to female royalty and pint-sized Australian singers. Sussex itself boasts a wealth of locations with 'bottom' in the name and this walk offers you the chance to visit a few and indulge in some fruity innuendos with your fellow walkers. And what a rollicking good walk this is too: the stately charm of Stanmer Park, the imposing contours of the South Downs, beautiful views, pretty woodland trails, and even a few eccentric curios such as the mysterious grave of a dead dog. Do be aware that this walk is quite hilly in places, so don't be surprised if you end up with tired thighs. And possibly a little arse-ache.

 Bus 78 from the Clock Tower takes you right into the park and drops you by the church

 8 miles/4 hours

 Stanmer village bus stop

 Car park on the left just after the bus stop

 Some fairly steep hills

 17th century dew ponds, ice cream van, large green bottoms

 Having your ears blown off by the wind on the Downs 40%

 The Wicker Man

① Alight from the bus at Stanmer village, or if driving go into the park, pass Stanmer House on your left, turn right past the church and find the car park just after the bus stop on your left. Go into the village by passing a massive old barn on your right, and canter up the main street.

Stanmer village is miniscule, yet perfectly formed to evoke the chocolate box image of ye olde English country life. There are picturesque cottages with a dash of wisteria, a horse in a field, a tearoom and the pervading aroma of cow dung.

② At the end of the houses turn right to a gate and go steeply uphill across a field. As the field opens out go diagonally left and up towards the woods. There are two gates available through the fence about a hundred yards apart; take the right hand one. Follow the path straight into the woods, ignore a minor crossroads and, a hundred yards on at a proper crossroads, go left. After another few hundred yards with the woods thinning out on your right, go through a gate on your right and go half left into a square meadow bordered by trees on all sides. Head for the gate in the opposite corner. Back in woods again, follow the path straight and slightly downhill. Where it bends left, we're going to leave the path briefly by crashing through the last few yards of undergrowth to the edge of the open land in front of you. Don't worry, we'll return to the path in a jiffy.

Almost directly ahead in the valley there's a mound the size of a small hill – these are quite common and colloquially referred to as 'chesty lumps'. In fact they are round barrows, piles of earth and stone placed over burial chambers. This particular one is Bronze Age. Or possibly Neolithic. Or it could be one of the Saxon ones. Or a Viking. Anyway it's jolly old.

③ Return to the path and follow it, keeping the open country to your right. Shortly you'll see the ground to your right start to slope steeply away, and through the trees you'll see that you're walking along the edge of a long valley. This is Moon's Bottom.

Moon's Bottom provides extra value with its dual innuendo, so have an additional suppressed snort as you peer into its crack.

④ The path joins another from the right and then quickly meets a crossroads. Take a moment to enjoy the tree trunk of carved woodland creatures, then turn right down the hill. At the bottom you'll come to a gate. Peek to your right and you'll see the end of Moon's Bottom. Then plunge sharp left into the woods towards another gate 50 yards away. Ignore this gate and instead head to its right through vegetation and over rotting tree trunks for about 100 yards (keeping as close as you can to the wire fence), until you find another small gate on your left that leads into an open field. Yes, it is a bit confusing but perseverance will pay off and you'll be proud at having strayed from the proverbial path.

⑤ Go through this gate and turn right along the field edge, with woodland and a fence to your right. After several hundred yards there's another gate to go through, at which point a path is visible leading diagonally left up the slope in front of you towards open country. Follow this up onto and then along the ridge. At this point the Downs

suddenly opens up all around you, providing breathtaking views of hills and troughs in all directions. At the end of the ridge you'll come to a fence blocking your path, with a gate in the middle and a huge almost circular valley visible beyond.Yes, I'm afraid you're going straight down there and then up the the other side. I know I know, you'd have gone to the Lake District if you wanted to do this kind of 'performance' walking. What's that, your bad knee's suddenly started playing you up and you'll have to go back the other way? And you can see a lot of fierce looking cows down there? Don't be a wuss, it won't take long and you can have an ice cream when you get there.

This vast and rather beautiful valley is called Big Bottom, its name a tribute to width rather than length. The entire contour is actually rather pleasingly buttock-shaped. Up on the next ridge at the opposite corner of what is essentially one big field lies Ditchling Beacon car park, so on a sunny day you should be able to spot the merry twinkle of laminated safety windscreens.

⑥ Up the other side of Big Bottom you'll find a dew pond, a stile to hop over and a dangerous lane to cross. It's got excitement this walk, you can't deny it.

Dew ponds are like little bottoms cut into the high ground and then, contrary to their name, allowed to fill with rainwater rather than dew. On an entirely unrelated note, the word 'dewlap' is old Sussex dialect for an early morning spider's web. Such moisture traps were considered useful if you'vd gone off to work in the fields in the morning and forgotten your thermos of cider.

⑦ Take care crossing the road to the small car park opposite as there's a blind bend to your right and frequent traffic. In the car park itself there's often an ice cream van (even on days when it's snowing) so reward yourself for the mega-climb with a 99. If it isn't there, go back to the dew pond and have a thirst-quenching slurp of genuine 17th century rainwater. Carry on through the car park, through a gate, and follow the ridge west.

Ditchling Beacon, sitting directly above Ditchling village which is down below the ridge to the north, was named for its use as one of the fire sites warning of the approach of the Spanish Armada. There's still a few fires lit up here even now, although we're not sure whether we should count people having drunken barbecues. You'll also find a fair few of the aforementioned chesty lumps along here.

⑧ Keep along the ridge for half a mile through a couple of gates, until you pass a dew pond on your left. Opening up beyond the pond is Dencher Bottom, which you pass on your left as another dew pond (Burnt House Pond) hoves into view on the right.

Dencher Bottom was one of the last intact chalk grasslands to be ploughed up in the 1950s. However it may look now, all of the Downs has been subjected to this indignity at some point during the last 150 years. This is a good spot for hares, purse-web spiders and boxing gloves spiders. The latter aren't much use in a ruck since their 'gloves' just dangle there like a tiny pair of ripe melons.

⑨ Go through two more gates, and you'll see a finger post (the 'Keymer Post') on your right. Follow its pointy finger left towards Brighton, down the edge of a mangel-wurzel field. Halfway down the hill at the field corner hop over a stile to the left and continue down to the bottom in the adjacent field. Go over another stile and turn left down a track that passes through a farm.

⑩ Stay on the track as it bends right and look for a stony track to your left with a waymark. Turn left uphill towards a lonely-looking barn, follow the track round the back of this and go over a stile. Follow the edge of the field anti-clockwise, ignoring

the next stile, until you reach a dew pond and the road.

As you ascend towards the road, down to your right is Eastwick Bottom. Despite there being an Iron Age field system buried under here, much of the topography has been created by the vast piles of chalk dumped during construction of the Brighton bypass in the early 90s. Recent archaeological digging revealed an extremely rare VHS tape of the first Teenage Mutant Ninja Turtles film.

⑪ Cross the road and then a short stretch of grass, and turn right onto a path running parallel with the road. Follow it as it enters woodland and after a while crosses a metalled lane. Take the second right of the paths immediately after the lane (it's pretty much straight on) and continue through the woods for ten minutes to a small car park. There's a confusing multiplicity of paths here, but the one you want is the second on the left, just after the start of the banking that surrounds the cars, that descends and then bends off to the right. At the bottom you'll find a metal gate and a sign forbidding entry. Turn right along the path that runs flat past a long wall and orchard on your left. Just before the path reaches open grass there is a green metal post, and a couple of yards before that is the marked tomb of a murdered dog.

This small pet graveyard lies in what were formerly the gardens and grounds of Stanmer House, which was the status of most of today's park. Have a rummage in the bushes and you should discover at least two more gravestones of long expired animals. Sadly, history does not record the precise nature of the unfortunate dog Snow's premature demise when he was "killed at Hollambury" but top detectives who worked on the case believe he was definitely a white dog with a dyslexic owner.

⑫ Turn left out of the woods and find the path that runs close along the right of the greenhouses. Turn right as you emerge onto a road and if it's open (some Thursday and Friday mornings and summer Sunday afternoons) pay a visit to the rural museum where ancient wise men will be able to advise you on the best way to get a solid day's work out of a donkey. They also provide a guided tour of an old gypsy caravan used for newlyweds. It's more fun that it sounds, honest. Continue down the road to return to your start point and, if you're hungry, you can look forward to a good plate of nosh at the Stanmer village tearoom. You've forgotten where it is? It's right next to the barn full of buttocks. I mean bullocks. Sorry, couldn't resist.

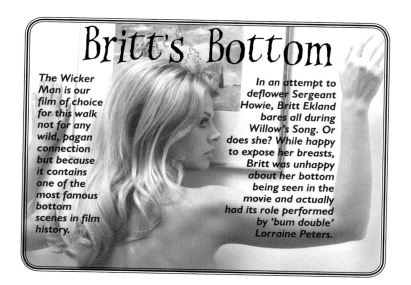

Britt's Bottom

The Wicker Man is our film of choice for this walk not for any wild, pagan connection but because it contains one of the most famous bottom scenes in film history.

In an attempt to deflower Sergeant Howie, Britt Ekland bares all during Willow's Song. Or does she? While happy to expose her breasts, Britt was unhappy about her bottom being seen in the movie and actually had its role performed by 'bum double' Lorraine Peters.

THE PERFECT WALK

Imagine, if you will, dipping a chocolate Hobnob into a piping hot mug of tea, having your feet massaged and watching your favourite sitcom all at the same time. Even if you prefer Jaffa Cakes, this walk is easily on a par with such moments of perfection and joy. Unless of course it's chucking it down. Starting and ending in the absurdly picturesque town of Arundel, it wanders by whispering reeds, wooded glades, a fine village cricket field and two country pubs, before ushering you into a riverside tea garden for a jammy scone. What's more, there aren't even any hills; it's all flat and lovely, like Morrissey's singing. Full of romance and adventure, this is *the* walk for popping the big question to your loved one or bringing a visitor from the Colonies, just for the pleasure of nonchalantly saying, "Oh look, a castle," when the stunning Arundel Castle first comes in sight. And as the walk ends in Arundel itself, you can round off a perfect day slurping Earl Grey, perusing the shops and castle or hiring a motorboat to head off down the River Arun in search of mischief.

 Train from Brighton Station or Hove to Arundel, changing at Barnham or Ford

 8.5 miles/4 hours

 Arundel rail station

 Rail station car park

 Flat and grassy

 Kingfishers, dormice, castle, meadows & the rare boss-eyed Dusseldorf Duck at the Arundel Wildfowl Centre

 Death by cream-tea related heart attack 8%

 The Princess Bride

① Walk towards the town centre along the Causeway (which becomes Queen Street). Immediately before the bridge turn right at a public footpath sign. This shortly turns left through a small car park and leads you onto the East bank of the River Arun, where you turn right. The path continues along the bank for around a mile, past Arundel Boat Yard.

Despite being a few miles inland, Arundel was once a significant port able to accommodate 200 ton tall ships packed to the brim with jam, tea towels, jam, knitwear and jam, ready for export. This was due to the Arun's big tidal range, making it appear full to the brim or three quarters empty at times. It is also very fast flowing, so don't even think about going for a paddle. Like wild animals and celebrities it is best admired from a distance.

② The path eventually veers right, away from the river, through a kissing gate, towards a white house and the railway line. Cross the line then, after the white house, turn left *immediately*. Though the path initially looks like it belongs to the house, don't worry, you won't end up in someone's kitchen having to pretend you've come to fix the Aga.

③ The path soon passes through a wooded area after which there is a kissing gate. Go through, and ignoring the stile on the right, continue left on the main path, which is bordered by trees on the left and a fence on the right. Where the fence and trees run out, go over the stile at the end of the path and head diagonally right across the field. Cross the small bridge and after around 50 yards go left over the stile and walk the 200 yards or so to the riverbank (which may just look like marsh and reeds), where you turn right.

④ The path continues along the bank for a while, over some stiles then heads right towards a wooded area, immediately before which is another stile. Cross the stile and follow the stepped path, which leads up through the trees. At the top follow the path left, which after a couple of hundred yards brings you to Burpham village cricket field. Skirt its edge, past the pavilion, just after which is The George pub and the village centre.

It's hard to improve on a hot summer Sunday afternoon spent watching the village team knocking up the runs, while you gently nod off. Even better, however, is a slap-up pub lunch, and despite being on a winding road to just about nowhere the community-owned George is pretty popular and serves excellent food. It was also voted 'Number 1 Pub to Walk to' by Daily Telegraph readers, which is a little baffling as we all know that they only ever travel by horse or Range Rover.

⑤ After the pub continue straight ahead into the churchyard. Pass to the left of the church and through the metal gate out of the yard onto the road, where you turn right. Continue along the road until you reach Peppering Farm then continue straight ahead along the track signposted 'Public Bridleway' passing to the right of the barn. The path undulates then descends, eventually passing through trees. Go left over the second stile, which is opposite a small chalk cliff.

⑥ The path skirts the edge of the field to the right of a drainage ditch. At the end of the field cross the next stile over some water. The path forks here; head right through the trees which after about a mile end at a stile, where you turn left along a track. The path eventually rises towards a gate, where it meets

a road. Turn left down the road (ignoring the descending right fork) and walk the few hundred yards down towards the hamlet of North Stoke.

⑦ Immediately before entering North Stoke, take the public footpath that is signposted to the left (if you pass the phone box, you have gone too far). The path descends across a field, through a kissing gate, into a wooded area and across an unusual wooden suspension bridge. Continue through the trees for a few hundred yards, then through the kissing gate and up to the riverbank, where you turn left towards the bridge. *After the bridge look out for the carved tree seat. It's customary to sit here, munch on a packet of prawn cocktail crisps and make a wish. We have no idea what the letters AMMHNA stand for though we did waste an entire afternoon trying to think of something suitably silly.*

⑧ Cross the bridge then turn left down the riverbank. The path continues along the bank for around two miles, eventually giving you great views of Arundel Castle.

So perfectly do the castle and town conform to fantasy stereotype that

you could easily believe yourself to be approaching an American theme park called Englandland. The castle is indeed too good to be true. Its present day facade is largely the late 19th century creation of the 14th Duke of Norfolk, who'd obviously watched one too many Disney films. The current Duke, the 18th, also has the titles 14th Earl of Arundel, 19th Earl of Surrey, 16th Earl of Norfolk, 13th Baron Beaumont, 26th Baron Maltravers, 16th Baron FitzAlan, 16th Baron Clun, 16th Baron Oswaldestre, 5th Baron Howard of Glossop, Earl Marshal, Hereditary Marshal of England and, best of all, Chief Butler of England. But his friends just call him Ken.

⑨ Eventually the path veers right, away from the river, over a stile, then left through trees and into the car park of The Black Rabbit pub for your second pub lunch.

The Black Rabbit's idyllic riverside location does mean it can be ridiculously busy. However, outside of peak hours a table by the river can still feel like heaven. You might wish to take a detour at this point to the Wildfowl & Wetlands Trust, which is just down the road from the pub. As well as endless species of wildfowl, it's home to a growing population of dormice.

⑩ After the pub the riverside path resumes and follows the meandering Arun for a further mile back to the tea gardens in Arundel town centre for cream tea and your third meal.

Waterside Tea Garden has another great riverfront location. Sure, you could have a sandwich, but this place was made for cream teas. Once you've clogged your arteries why not spend your final moments on earth on a motorboat? Four and six seaters can be hired from the office next door or you could take a three-hour cruise further up the river. Don't forget to pack a few chocolate eclairs in case you get peckish.